TRAINING PARAPROFESSIONALS FOR REFERENCE SERVICE

A How-To-Do-it Manual
For Librarians

JULIE ANN McDANIEL
JUDITH K. OHLES

*HOW-TO-DO-IT MANUALS
FOR LIBRARIES*

Number 30

NEAL-SCHUMAN PUBLISHERS, INC.
New York, London

Published by Neal-Schuman Publishers, Inc.
100 Varick Street
New York, NY 10013

Printed and bound in the United States of America

Library of Congress Cataloging-in-Publication Data

McDaniel, Julie Ann.
    Training paraprofessionals for reference service : a how-to-do-it
manual for librarians / Julie Ann McDaniel and Judith K. Ohles.
        p.   cm. -- (How-to-do-it manuals for libraries : no. 30)
    Includes bibliographical references and index.
    ISBN 1-55570-084-5
    1. Reference services (Libraries)--Study and teaching--United
States. 2. Library technicians--Training of--United States.
I. Ohles, Judith K. II. Title. III. Series.
Z711.2.M36   1993
025.5'2'071173--dc20   93-9883
                                                           CIP

TO LIBRARY PARAPROFESSIONALS

CONTENTS

PREFACE

Adding paraprofessionals to a library's reference staff can be a great help for overburdened reference desks. Paraprofessionals can help maximize reference services by providing extra hours of service, depth of coverage, or both—but they must be trained well in order to be effective. Everyone who works at a reference desk needs training and paraprofessionals are no exception.

In *Training Paraprofessionals for Reference Service*, we provide a step-by-step plan for preparing paraprofessionals for reference service. We begin with the planning stages and discuss the importance of developing a departmental manual for the use of all staff, but especially for new staff. We move next to the all-important step of orientation—how to help the new paraprofessional begin to feel comfortable in the position. Then we cover the vital elements of reference work, the reference interview and reference sources. We discuss methods for teaching paraprofessionals when and how to conduct reference interviews, and we provide sample training modules to help you learn how to prepare vital and efficient paraprofessional training sessions. Finally, we cover the evaluation of paraprofessionals and revision of the training program you have developed for your library.

This plan has been tested in the real world—we have used it and know that it works. By using the information and tools we have provided, you can create and carry out a successful training program to add effective paraprofessionals to your reference staff.

ACKNOWLEDGMENTS

We would like to thank the following people for their assistance with the book:

Dr. James W. Geary of Kent State University, who suggested that we write this book.

Our supervisors, who gave us necessary support, encouragement, and freedom in creating and implementing training programs: Martha Goold and Barbara F. Schloman of Kent State University, and Judith M. Pask of Purdue University.

Those who provided assistance in collecting materials: Laura Harlow, Timothy Addison, and Audra Ezell of the Purdue University Undergraduate Library, and Sarah J. Cook and Lin Ng of the Ohio Wesleyan University Libraries; Elizabeth Rausch of the Purdue University Undergraduate Library, for assistance in typing bibliographies; and Dr. Lynda K. Hall, of Ohio Wesleyan University, for reviewing the Training Reaction Survey.

The staffs of the following libraries: Kent State University Libraries Interlibrary Loan Department, Ohio Wesleyan University Libraries Interlibrary Loan Department, Purdue University Libraries Interlibrary Loan Department, Stark County District Library Periodicals Department, and Walsh College Library.

The Kent State University Reference Committee on Student Utilization and Training (comprised of Dr. James W. Geary, chair; Julia Canan, Ruth Main, and Judy Ohles), for some preliminary ideas.

Eleanor Byerly, Sarah Cook, Mary Gaylord, Maureen Kilcullen, Kara Robinson, Jane Slosser, and Tim McDaniel, for their encouragement and advice.

1 INTRODUCTION

Chapter Overview

- Why Use Paraprofessionals?
- Why Not Use Paraprofessionals?
- Making the decision

"Choosing to use nonprofessionals in the reference area is neither all good nor all bad, as is true for most management decisions. The actual balance between good and bad depends on conditions at each library."

Nancy Emmick, "Nonprofessionals on Reference Desks in Academic Libraries," in *Conflicts in Reference Services*, Bill Katz and Ruth A. Fraley, eds. New York: The Haworth Press, 1985.

WHAT'S IN A NAME?

Many terms are used for non-MLS library workers, some of which are roughly synonymous with the term "paraprofessional." These include support staff, paralibrarians, aides, assistants, and technicians. The term preprofessional is sometimes used for paraprofessionals who are working towards attaining the MLS degree. Some libraries also use the term "subprofessional" or "nonprofessional" to distinguish librarians from other staff, but these terms have the disadvantages of being both too generic and somewhat negative in tone.

Reference librarians today are involved in a number of activities. In addition to staffing the reference desk, their responsibilities may include online searching, bibliographic instruction, collection development, committee work, program planning, supervision, research and publication, and special projects. Despite this increasing workload, library staff often desire to expand types and hours of service to help meet their patrons' needs. To do this, they must consider alternative methods for providing reference service. One such alternative is to hire paraprofessionals to staff the reference desk, thereby freeing reference librarians for other duties.

Once paraprofessionals are hired, they must receive training. Busy librarians and administrators may not realize the importance of training, or they may not have sufficient time available to develop training programs. Nevertheless, only with proper training can paraprofessionals provide the quality of service for which libraries strive. The time you spend in training paraprofessionals to staff the reference desk will ultimately pay off with increased levels and quality of service, improved staff morale, and better staff participation in the department's goals.

Before you hire paraprofessionals, you need to plan for the use of these new employees. You should determine the needs of your specific library and develop a plan for hiring, training, supervising, and evaluating paraprofessionals. Only then will they be ready to provide reference service. This chapter will cover:

- A definition of the term *paraprofessional*
- A discussion of why to use paraprofessionals
- The pros and cons related to using paraprofessionals in reference service.

The rest of the manual will help you design a training program for paraprofessionals who provide reference services in your library.

The prefix *para* means "by the side of." For example, paramedics or paralegals work with medical and legal professionals. In libraries, the word *paraprofessional* generally refers to an employee who does not have a Master of Library Science (MLS) degree, but who has been trained to work alongside a professional librarian. Paraprofessional will be the term used throughout this book to refer to library employees who do not have an MLS.

WHY USE PARAPROFESSIONALS?

Librarian Burnout: A variety of reasons exist for using paraprofessionals at the reference desk. Some studies have estimated that as many as 80 percent of the questions asked at reference desks do not require professional attention. Many of the questions asked at reference desks are directional or ready reference type questions. Paraprofessionals can be trained to answer the bulk of these repetitive or simple questions, and to refer more difficult questions to librarians, thus allowing librarians to use their professional skills more effectively. Obviously this requires spending time during training discussing, observing, and practicing the reference interview.

Individual Assistance for Patrons: Using paraprofessionals for reference service enables libraries to continue offering individual assistance at reference desks while expanding services in other areas. Activities such as online searching, bibliographic instruction, and collection development require librarians to be away from the reference desk. Requirements for faculty status (research, publication, teaching) may mean fewer hours at the reference desk for many professional academic reference librarians.

Increased Service Hours: Paraprofessionals at the reference desk can enable the library to offer more hours of reference service. Libraries can use paraprofessionals to provide early morning, late night, and weekend desk coverage. In some libraries, if there were no paraprofessionals to work these hours, no reference service would be available. Other libraries schedule paraprofessionals to work at the same time librarians work so that more patrons can be served during busier times.

Expanded Subject Expertise: Paraprofessionals can also expand the subject base of the reference department. Many librarians have undergraduate degrees in the humanities, leaving some reference departments with a lack of subject expertise in other fields. One way to have subject specialists in the hard sciences and social sciences is to hire people without library degrees but with valuable subject area knowledge.

WHY NOT USE PARAPROFESSIONALS?

Value of Professional Education: In many libraries, when there is enough money, entry-level librarians are hired to staff the reference desk, but when money is scarce libraries often turn to paraprofessionals for reference staffing. This could send an erroneous message that librarianship is not absolutely committed to its professional degree. Ideally, paraprofessionals should be hired only to complement, not replace, professional librarians, but, regrettably, this is not always the case. Nevertheless, it is imperative that libraries that choose to hire paraprofessionals for reference service provide adequate training so that patron service does not suffer.

Reference Interview: Opponents of using paraprofessionals at the reference desk assert that paraprofessionals often cannot recognize when a reference interview is needed, or if they do, do not know how to conduct one. Some librarians believe paraprofessionals are afraid to try to answer difficult questions so they accept simple ones at face value.

Incorrect Referrals: Librarians also argue that paraprofessionals often do not make referrals or do not recognize when to make a referral to a professional. Of course, if paraprofessionals often work alone on evenings or weekends, there may not be anyone in the building to whom they can refer or with whom they can consult. Some librarians argue that professional librarians should receive all questions and refer to paraprofessionals rather than expect the paraprofessional to decide when a referral is necessary. Other librarians believe paraprofessionals can be so eager to help they will not refer to or consult with a librarian. The difficulty of supervising reference work gives rise to concern about the success of the reference interview and referrals. Cataloging or interlibrary loan work can be double-checked and corrected if necessary before it leaves the department. Reference service, however, does not lend itself to close supervision or correction. The immediate and individual nature of reference work makes it almost impossible to ensure that every question is answered correctly. If a professional librarian must be assigned to watch every transaction in which a paraprofessional is involved, nothing has been gained. However, if the paraprofessional is allowed to answer questions without training, the quality of service may be lowered because of faulty reference interviewing, incorrect referrals, or simply wrong answers. Some libraries may choose to set up guidelines governing the use of paraprofessionals at reference desks. For example, policy may be written requiring that para-professionals always work with a librarian, or that the librarian receive all questions and then refer appropriate questions to the paraprofessional for handling. Paraprofessionals may be allowed to answer only directional or ready reference questions, or they may be asked to get a patron started and then confer with a librarian to determine if the complete, correct answer was given. Guidelines such as these can help avoid incorrect referrals.

Training Time: Training and supervising paraprofessionals takes a great deal of time, which can decrease the amount of time librarians have for online searches, collection development, bib-liographic instruction, meeting faculty status requirements, and other activities. Because of this, using paraprofessionals can sometimes be too time-consuming to be worthwhile—profession-als may not really gain more time to spend on activities other than the reference desk. In libraries where the paraprofessional staff is small and has a low rate of turnover, the hiring and training of paraprofessionals will be infrequent and less time-consuming. In libraries with larger staffs and high turnover, one librarian may need to devote some or all of his or her time to training and supervising paraprofessionals.

High Turnover: Paraprofessionals who take a library position only until they can obtain higher level jobs or work in the subject fields, may not stay long enough to justify their training. With no standardization of job titles among libraries, opportunities for paraprofessionals to move to similar positions in other libraries may be limited and possibilities for promotion within a given institution without obtaining an MLS degree may be nonexistent. High turnover can greatly increase the time spent in the selecting and training process for the library.

MAKING THE DECISION

Despite the arguments against the practice, many libraries realize that using paraprofessionals is an effective way of maximizing their reference services. Many of the risks of using paraprofessionals can be eliminated or greatly diminished through proper selection and training. Concerns about faulty reference interviews and lack of experience with reference sources can be overcome if the library hires the right individuals and then trains them well. It is important to realize, however, that this requires a considerable amount of planning and effort from the library's professional staff.

Each library must finally come to its own conclusions about using paraprofessionals at its reference desk. The library must decide whether the benefits—adding subject depth, increasing service hours, freeing its professional staff for other work, or some combination—are worth the investment required to select and train paraprofessionals. Each library must also decide what levels of questions it believes are appropriate for paraprofessionals to answer and how much education the position should require.

Ultimately, it is the professional librarians who are responsible for the service offered in their library. Librarians must accept responsibility for the training paraprofessionals receive and the service paraprofessionals provide. Paraprofessionals who work at the reference desk cannot be expected to learn only by observation. They need carefully planned training to orient them to the library, to familiarize them with library philosophy, policies and procedures, and to guide them in the use of reference sources and the reference interview. Without this training, paraprofessionals will not be able to provide high quality service at the reference desk and will not become fully contributing members of the department.

RESOURCES

Christensen, John O., Larry D. Benson, H. Juliene Butler, Blaine H. Hall, and Don H. Howard. "An Evaluation of Reference Desk Service." *College and Research Libraries* 50 (July 1989): 468-483. An unobtrusive test was conducted to assess the effectiveness of the paraprofessional staffing used at the reference desk at Brigham Young University Lee Library. The training program was found to be ineffective because student assistants answered only 36 percent of the questions correctly.

Emmick, Nancy. "Nonprofessionals on Reference Desks in Academic Libraries." In *Conflicts in Reference Services*, edited by Bill Katz and Ruth A. Fraley, 149-160. New York: The Haworth Press, 1985. Emmick reviews the responsibilities of academic reference librarians and then examines the role paraprofessionals can play at the reference desk, with an overview of arguments for and against their use.

Montag, John. "Choosing How to Staff the Reference Desk." In *Personnel Issues in Reference Services*, edited by Bill Katz and Ruth A. Fraley, 31-37. New York: The Haworth Press, 1986. Montag discusses items to consider when deciding to use paraprofessionals in reference service including local choice, quality of service, training, education, staffing, personnel policies, salaries, and equity.

Murfin, Marjorie. "Trends in Use of Support Staff and Students at the Reference Desk in Academic Libraries." *Library Personnel News* 2 (Winter 1988): 10-12. Murfin considers arguments for and against the use of paraprofessionals and predicts that a reference team concept will develop in which professionals will suggest subject headings, sources, and search strategy while paraprofessionals would handle directional questions, be responsible for equipment, and assist patrons in the searches initiated by professionals.

Murfin, Marjorie E., and Charles A. Bunge. "Paraprofessionals at the Reference Desk." *The Journal of Academic Librarianship* 14 (March 1988): 10-14. Murfin and Bunge tested patron satisfaction in 20 academic libraries and found that patrons who dealt with paraprofessionals at reference desks were consistently and significantly unsatisfied with the service they received. Murfin and Bunge found several behaviors exhibited by paraprofessionals that increased patron satisfaction.

Woodard, Beth S. "The Effectiveness of an Information Desk Staffed by Graduate Students and Nonprofessionals." *College and Research Libraries* 50 (July 1989): 455-467. Woodard reports on an unobtrusive test done at the University of Illinois in Urbana-Champaign where paraprofessionals staff an information desk. They found that 62 percent of the questions were being answered correctly and that staffing level affected paraprofessional performance.

2 PLANNING

Because more and more paraprofessionals are staffing reference desks, the quality of their training is extremely important. To ensure effective training, supervisors must plan for it. Proper planning will help ensure that library goals are met, reduce uncertainty for all library staff members, and, in the long run, save time.

A written training plan is useful for both the supervisor and the new employee. Written plans may include training checklists; a calendar of training activities; a detailed summary of what will be covered, by whom, and with what resources; or a combination of any of these. Once a training plan has been developed, it must be implemented, tested for effectiveness, and revised when necessary. Although developing an effective training plan takes time, once the plan is in place, the training process is easier for trainers, trainees, and supervisors alike. Employees benefit from training plans by knowing what is expected of them and when, and by understanding the sequence and content of the training.

This chapter will cover aspects of planning for training: creating a job description; identifying training needs; establishing goals and objectives for a training program; sequencing of training; and determining who will handle paraprofessional training.

JOB DESCRIPTION

Before using paraprofessionals for reference service, library administrators need to decide exactly why paraprofessionals are needed and what they will be asked to do. Are they needed during busy times or for late night or evening hours? Will they work alone or will they always be scheduled to work with a reference librarian? Will they be trained to answer any and all questions that come up, or will they be expected to handle only ready reference or directional questions? Will paraprofessionals only provide assistance at the reference desk, or will they have other responsibilities to carry out when patrons do not need assistance? Where will the paraprofessional be located in the reference center and how will patrons know to approach the paraprofessional? These questions and many others should be taken into consideration before hiring paraprofessionals.

Obviously, the new employee cannot be told, "Just help this librarian." The employee will be left wondering what exactly is expected, and the librarian will also have questions. Is the paraprofessional to select books? Answer all questions? Type book orders? Prepare reports? Other staff members may also question why the paraprofessional was hired and how the work of the new employee will affect their responsibilities.

It is useful to ask each member of the reference staff to make a list of the tasks that he or she believes a paraprofessional should be asked to handle. The department can then meet to review the lists and select the most appropriate tasks. These should be described as precisely as possible, using active words and avoiding vague phrases like "sometimes" or "could be asked to." This list can then be turned into a job description, which will be used to develop the training plan, and as the basis for the job advertisement and the evaluation form.

A job description identifies the responsibilities performed and qualifications required for a specific job. The job description should specify as many of the required tasks of the job as possible, but is not expected to include everything. In addition to describing the work to be done, it should indicate what qualifications such as education, experience, and skills are necessary to successfully perform the job. It may also describe qualifications that are desirable, but not necessary. A job announcement is a condensed version of the job description and is primarily used for advertising job openings.

Without a written job description to guide them, it will be difficult to hire, train, supervise, or evaluate paraprofessionals. The job description will be used to design the training program. For example, a paraprofessional who is asked to conduct online searches needs an introduction to online searching during the training program. The job description will also help identify the responsibilities of the supervisors and provide criteria for evaluation of the paraprofessionals. Finally, job descriptions help the paraprofessional understand the requirements and expectations of the position.

WRITING THE JOB DESCRIPTION

The following items should be considered when writing job descriptions, although the arrangement of them can be decided by each library. Sample descriptions are given in Figures 2-1, 2-2, 2-3.

Figure 2-1

SAMPLE JOB DESCRIPTION

REFERENCE ASSISTANT

Assists patrons in locating library materials through the use of the library catalog and printed indexes.

Responds to patron information needs through the use of reference sources.

Checks in and shelves magazines.

Operates, explains, maintains, and orders supplies for library photocopier, micro-film reader/printer, and microfiche reader/printer.

Other responsibilities as needed.

Part-time, 15–20 hours per week. After school and early evening hours and some Saturday mornings. Reports to Reference Librarian.

Must have completed high school. Should like people, enjoy a quiet workplace, be good with machines.

$_____ per hour.

Figure 2-2

SAMPLE JOB DESCRIPTION

LIBRARY AIDE

Duties:

Answers phone, mail, and in person reference questions in consultation with librarian.

Provides library introductions to local school and community groups.

Prepares reference materials for use.

Supervises Reference Department shelver.

Writes monthly book review column for local newspaper.

Plans exhibits for library lobby.

Supervised by Head of Reference.

Applicant must:

Have a bachelor's degree.

Be a resident of Cityville.

Be able to communicate effectively orally and in writing.

Be available to work some evenings and weekends.

Compensation:

Extensive training program.

$____ per hour; excellent benefits package.

Stimulating work environment.

Figure 2-3

SAMPLE JOB DESCRIPTION

SCIENCE SPECIALIST

Description:

Assists library patrons in a busy academic science library.

Duties:

Twenty hours per week is spent at the reference desk of the Science Library, which primarily serves graduate students and faculty members actively involved in research. Offdesk duties: prepares bibliographies as needed by library patrons; assists in selection of materials for the science reference collection; serves as liaison to one academic department to coordinate book purchases for collection.

Reports to:

Head of Science Library.

Education:

M.S. in physical sciences, math, or computer science.

Experience:

No library experience is required.

Working conditions:

The Science Specialist must be able to quickly find information needed by researchers who are often unable to visit the library in person.

Salary:

$_____, dependent on experience; tuition and health benefits.

Job Title: Select a descriptive, unambiguous title for the position.

Purpose of the Job: This should be a single sentence describing the job. It should highlight the most important responsibilities to be carried out by the paraprofessional.

Responsibilities: List the tasks for which the paraprofessional will be responsible. Duties should be listed in their order of importance. Do not include procedures for accomplishing the tasks; these should be included in the training manual. Ideally, positions should have between three and five primary responsibilities. These should be similar enough so that they require the same level of education, experience, and skills. It may be wise to end this section with the phrase "other duties as required." This phrase allows you to increase the responsibilities for the position if the paraprofessional you hire proves to be capable of handling more than the original job description details. Furthermore, if changes occur in the library, such as a reorganization or the introduction of new technology, the responsibilities of the paraprofessional might need to be changed. The phrase "other duties as required" provides flexibility for such situations.

Reports To: Indicate to whom the paraprofessional will be responsible. This is needed to help all staff members understand where the position fits into the organizational structure of the library. If any other employees will be reporting to the person who holds the position, it should also be noted in this section.

Qualifications: In this section, identify the education, skills, and experience that you know are needed and those that you believe are desirable to do the job. Federal laws against discriminatory hiring require that employers be able to prove that employment requirements are necessary for the successful completion of the job. Consult a lawyer or human resources professional if you have any questions about the legality of a particular requirement.

> Education: Indicate the minimum amount of education needed to successfully perform the job. If a degree is necessary, indicate the particular subject specialty required or desired.

Experience: Indicate any experience that might be needed to perform the job. Make sure required experience is truly relevant for the job. For example, clerical skills should not be required if the employee will never be asked to type or file.

Skills: Indicate any skills that are necessary for the job. You may need paraprofessionals who have good oral and written communication skills, or who can type or operate equipment such as copiers, computers, printers, or microfiche or microfilm machines.

Special Interests: If there are special interests that will help the employee perform the job, list them here. Depending on the type of position, desirable special interests might include genealogical research or local history, liking children, or enjoying trivia.

Working Conditions: This section is optional and includes any special information about the library and/or department that might be important to potential applicants. If evening or weekend work will be required, it should be noted. Some indication of the stress level of the job could also be given. For example, note if the reference area is often noisy or if there are usually many patrons waiting for assistance. Indicate if physical work, such as lifting heavy boxes or standing for long periods of time, will be required.

Salary: Indicate the wage or salary to be paid. Mention any benefits for which the paraprofessional will be eligible.

Job descriptions must be revised periodically. The library should establish a schedule for revising all of its job descriptions. New equipment in the department may require new or different skills than those identified in the original job description. Reorganization of the library or reference department may mean new responsibilities for the position that need to be included in the job description. Revision of the original description for the reference paraprofessional will be discussed further in Chapter 8 (Evaluation and Revision of the Training Program).

IDENTIFYING TRAINING NEEDS

After the job description is written, you can begin work on the training plan. Look at each task and list what the paraprofessional needs to know to accomplish that task.

As an example, think about the job description in Figure 2-1. The Reference Assistant will be asked to "assist patrons in locating library materials through the use of the library catalog and printed indexes." This obviously implies that the paraprofessional will need to know how to use the library's catalog and its printed indexes, but there are other less obvious training needs hidden in this task. The paraprofessional will also need to be trained in effective reference interviewing techniques, how to use the subject headings authority list, how to read a call number, how to use the library's periodical holdings list, how to request items from storage, and any number of other specific procedures and policies involved in using the collection. As you prepare a list of training needs, think of this fill in the blank sentence:

> To do _____, the paraprofessional needs to know _____ or understand _____.

This should help you think of policies and activities that affect the task to be done. Figure 2-4 provides a sample list of training needs for each task for the Reference Assistant.

Careful attention is needed in the planning stages to be sure that paraprofessionals are being taught everything they will need to know to do their job effectively. The training plan can be prepared by one person or a committee but, to ensure that everything is included, it should be reviewed by several people who were not responsible for its creation.

Other training policy issues that you need to address are limitations and guidelines for training, a training manual, and evaluation of job performance and of the training program. The latter two are discussed in Chapter 7, Performance Evaluation and Chapter 8, Training Evaluation and Revision. Limitations and guidelines for training should accommodate departmental priorities and paraprofessionals' experience and skills. They may include things such as the number of weeks spent on training, the primary focus of training (catalog assistance, ready reference questions, readers' advisory, etc.), and the amount of time devoted to attitudinal training.

OBJECTIVES

Objectives are useful because they provide:

- Consistency in the design of the training system.
- Effective communication.
- Assistance in selecting appropriate course content.
- Assistance in selecting the most suitable instructional strategy.
- Clearcut instructor and trainee goals.
- Basis for developing criterion measures.
- Performance standards.
- Objective evaluation of instruction.

Adapted from William R. Tracey. *Designing Training and Development Systems*. New York: AMACOM, 1984, 204-206.

THREE STEPS

Performance-centered objectives should:

Step 1. Identify the desired behavior.
Step 2. State the required conditions under which the behavior will be performed.
Step 3. State the criterion of acceptable performance.

For more information about writing objectives consult Robert Mager. *Preparing Instructional Objectives*. 2nd ed. Belmont, CA: Pitman Learning, 1975.

GOALS AND OBJECTIVES

Goals and objectives are formulated after the training needs are identified. Goals provide a broad description of an activity to be accomplished, while objectives identify each task that must be completed to reach the goal. A broad training goal might be that, after the completion of the training program, the paraprofessional will be a fully contributing member of the reference staff. Supervisors generally know what the desired outcome of training should be. It is important to write these outcomes, or goals, down. Written goals can be given to the paraprofessional and other reference staff members so that all employees are aware of what is expected.

In writing objectives, focus on paraprofessional performance. Acceptable performance levels and expected end results must be identified. Objectives must state the action that is to be performed and indicate how success will be measured. Each training need listed as a result of the duties in the job description should become a goal for the paraprofessional. Write objectives that identify the activities that must be carried out to meet that training need. For example:

> GOAL: Paraprofessional will be able to use the library catalog to assist patrons.

> OBJECTIVE: Given a main entry record, the paraprofessional will correctly identify all information in the record.

This objective:

> Provides us with a *task*: "identify information in the record";

> Indicates the *conditions* under which it will be performed: "given a main entry record" (not expected to do it from memory); and

> Tells us how to *measure* success: "all information" must be "correctly identified" (knowing the author, title, and call number would be insufficient).

In describing the activity to be performed, you should focus on the activity itself, not the instructional process. For instance, the following is an ineffective description: "After practicing looking

Figure 2-4

TRAINING NEEDS LIST: REFERENCE ASSISTANT

Task: Assists patrons in locating library materials through the use of the library catalog and printed indexes (see Figure 2-1).

Needs to know:

- Where things are in the library, emphasizing catalog area, index tables, periodical and book collections
- Understand library policy regarding circulation of periodicals
- Understand library policy regarding interlibrary loan
- How to conduct a reference interview
- How to use catalog
- How to use subject heading authority list (Sears or Library of Congress Subject Headings)
- How to read a call number
- How to use printed indexes
- How to use the library's periodicals holding list
- How to request items from storage

Task: Responds to patron information needs through the use of reference sources.

Needs to know:

- Where things are in the building, emphasizing reference area
- Understand library policies regarding amount of help given to each category of patrons
- How to conduct a reference interview
- What is in the reference collection
- What are the types of reference sources (almanacs, dictionaries etc.)
- How to use the local "hard to answer" file
- Understand to whom and how to refer difficult questions
- How to use the telephone system

Task: Checks in and shelves magazines.

Needs to know:
- Where things are in the building, emphasizing mail room, check-in area, and periodicals area
- How the periodical collection is arranged
- Understand library policy regarding turn around time
- Use of Cardex or check-in file
- How to stamp/label periodicals that are received
- How to claim periodicals not received

Task: Operates, explains, maintains, and orders supplies for library photocopier, microfilm reader/printer, and microfiche reader/printer.

Needs to know:
- Where things are in the building, emphasizing location of supplies and equipment
- How to use each piece of equipment
- How to order supplies
- Procedures for storing inventory/supply
- How to repair each piece of equipment
- Who to call for service for each piece of equipment
- How to handle money in each piece of equipment

ACTION WORDS

ask

define

demonstrate

describe

explain

identify

list

operate

refer

use

up subjects in a Wilson index, the paraprofessional will know how to use them."

This focuses on the instruction—practice—rather than on what the paraprofessional will be able to do after training. The activity should be described actively with *doing* words rather than *knowing* or *feeling* words. Words like *understand, appreciate, believe,* and *know* should be avoided. Instead try to use definitive action verbs such as *demonstrate, identify, list, describe,* and *explain.*

It is important to think about the action that the paraprofessional is expected to take when working with a patron. In some libraries, staff may demonstrate use of a source themselves, whereas in other libraries they may simply explain how to use a source and observe while the patron handles the book, turns pages, works through guide words, page numbers, and abbreviations. If the instructional objective indicates the type of service to be provided, the trainer can develop training with this in mind. Then the paraprofessional and training can be evaluated in light of this as well.

The second part of an instructional objective is the *conditions* under which an activity must be performed. Identifying the conditions that affect a specific service or task can provide guidance to the paraprofessional and other staff members about how it should be performed. There may be some activities that should routinely be conducted from memory—for example, recalling names of prominent authors, identifying general areas within a call number system, or giving directions to locations within the library. On the other hand, there may be activities for which paraprofessionals will be permitted or expected to refer to a source. Examples of these activities include consulting the library policy manual when answering questions related to the circulation policy, referring to printed materials when telling patrons how to dial into the library catalog, or using an almanac when answering certain reference questions. The instructional objectives for training should indicate whether the paraprofessional may, may not, or must refer to a specific source when doing the activity being learned.

When testing a paraprofessional to determine his or her level of understanding about a particular activity, it is important that the conditions of testing reflect the instructional objectives (which ideally reflect real life). In other words, after a training session about using a main entry record based on the sample objective above, it would be unfair to ask the paraprofessional to explain from memory the pieces of information included in a main entry.

There is no indication in the objective that the paraprofessional needs to respond to queries about main entries from memory. The objective indicates that the paraprofessional can and should refer to an actual record.

Finally, the objective should indicate how success will be *measured*. One possible measure of success is time. Some tasks may need to be performed within a certain amount of time. For example, finding a phone number in a phone book should generally take less than three minutes. However, it may not be possible or desirable to set time limits on some activities. For example, it would be very difficult to expect staff to meet an objective requiring them to explain to a patron in three minutes how to use the library's catalog. Additionally, it is probably undesirable to indicate to paraprofessionals that assistance should be provided according to time factors rather than patron need.

Another measure of success is accuracy. You might reasonably expect a paraprofessional to answer a specific percentage of all questions correctly and completely. While it is difficult to acknowledge that less than perfect reference service is acceptable, it is important to realize that no one is perfect. By setting a percentage lower than 100, you provide a goal for which the paraprofessional can strive as well as a reasonable guide for evaluating the success of training and the paraprofessional. An example:

> GOAL: Paraprofessional will be able to use printed indexes received by the library.
>
> OBJECTIVE: Given a copy of *Readers' Guide to Periodical Literature*, the paraprofessional will locate articles (or determine that none are included) on a given topic within five minutes.
>
> OBJECTIVE: Given a citation from *Readers' Guide to Periodical Literature*, the paraprofessional will correctly identify all parts of the citation.
>
> OBJECTIVE: Given the title and volume number of a periodical, the paraprofessional will correctly determine if it is available according to the library's periodical holdings list.

These three objectives break down the goal into manageable pieces, each of which is an important step in the process of using a periodical index. The first objective uses time as a measurement because the paraprofessional should be familiar enough with the arrangement of the index, its alphabetization scheme, and its cross references to determine if the topic is covered in the index. The second objective requires the paraprofessional to correctly identify the parts of a citation. You can easily measure the paraprofessional's ability to do this by asking him or her to name all of the parts of a citation. Remember that this does not have to be done from memory—our objective says "given a copy of *Readers' Guide*," which reasonably reflects a real life situation. Finally, the paraprofessional uses the periodical title and volume number to determine if the item is available locally by using the library's periodical holdings list.

Writing down the objectives is useful so that other staff can review them, make suggestions about their importance, and even suggest other topics that might also be covered. Paraprofessionals can also review the objectives before training begins to have an idea of what they will be expected to learn. Finally, written objectives are useful when training is completed so that you can review what was learned. It is easy to forget the goal of a training session if you have not thoroughly considered and written down your intentions.

Once the objectives are developed, the training needs list should be reviewed to ensure that each task that the paraprofessional will be asked to carry out has been accounted for in the goals and objectives you have written. Well-written objectives will provide a basis for determining training content, setting performance standards, and establishing staff expectations.

SEQUENCING

The last step in planning is usually deciding the proper sequence of training. The different training segments should start with something basic that can be built on with more and more advanced segments. The sequence of training should not be confusing to the paraprofessional.

There are three general principles behind effective sequencing of training:

1. Move from simple to complex
2. Begin segments with material that the trainees have already learned.

3. Allow trainees time to practice material learned from one segment before proceeding to other segments.

Basic tasks should be explained before more complex tasks are presented or tasks should be presented in the order that they are to be performed. When teaching a paraprofessional to use an online catalog, you should begin with author, title, or subject searches before progressing to Boolean logic or keyword searches. It is also useful to teach the paraprofessional how to do a search (make a menu choice or enter a command) before explaining how to move between screens or print a citation.

As a more complete example for our Reference Assistant (Figure 2-1), training related to using the library catalog would probably proceed in this order:

1. Tour of the building
2. Discussion of the purpose of the catalog
3. Explanation that every book is represented in the catalog at least once (main entry), possibly twice (main entry and title), or even more (main entry, title, and subject(s))
4. Demonstration of how to use the title section of the catalog
5. If needed, discussion of alphabetization practices
6. Discussion of how author's names are entered (last name, first name)
7. Demonstration of how to use the author section of the catalog
8. Discussion of subject heading authority lists
9. Explanation of cross reference procedures
10. Demonstration of how to use the subject section of the catalog

In this sequence, the paraprofessional becomes familiar with searching for titles first. Generally title searches will not involve cross references. This allows the paraprofessional to gain some confidence working with the catalog and seeing how the cards are arranged, or in the case of an online catalog, how the screens are displayed. Then the paraprofessional can move to author searching, which can involve navigating cross references. Finally the paraprofessional moves to subject searching, which can get quite complex with cross references and subject heading verification. By learning subject searching last, the paraprofessional should be somewhat comfortable with the catalog, its organization, and how it functions so that all that needs to be concentrated on is understanding the subject heading concepts. In this way, the training moved from a simple task—learning the catalog well enough to complete title searches—to a more complex task—understanding cross references—to the most complex task—complete subject searches. For further assistance with training related to library catalogs, see Chapter 6.

As part of sequencing, you need to plan how long training will take. It is best to have the paraprofessional begin with some time spent observing the reference desk and reference staff members as they answer reference questions. You will also need to decide how much time to devote to orientation (Chapter 4), the reference interview (Chapter 5), and instruction in using specific references and sources (Chapter 6). You will need to determine how quickly all of this can or needs to happen.

For many libraries and paraprofessionals, two to three weeks of observation during orientation and an initial discussion of the reference interview, followed by training related to one subject per week, will work well. The observation during orientation prepares the paraprofessional to answer directional questions. Initial discussion of the reference interview sensitizes the paraprofessional to the importance and potential difficulties involved. As the paraprofessional begins answering reference questions, he or she will appreciate the introduction to and in-depth examination of sources used to answer common reference questions.

CHOOSING THE TRAINER

Another consideration in the planning stages is deciding who will do the training. Training paraprofessionals takes a great deal of time, and the librarian assigned to the task may need to give up some other responsibilities while the training program is being designed and implemented. The library must be prepared to commit the personnel, time, and resources to the project to ensure that patrons receive quality service.

The characteristics required for an effective trainer are fairly obvious. Trainers should:

DESIRABLE TRAINER ABILITIES

- Takes an interest in the trainee.
- Creates enthusiasm.
- Keeps morale high.
- Communicates clearly.
- Listens.
- Provides feedback to the trainee in a timely and supportive manner (praise in public, correct in private).
- Recognizes the importance of self-confidence and self-esteem in the learning process.
- Understands learning principles.
- Recognizes the value of learning from mistakes.

From Sheila D. Creth. *Effective On-the-Job Training: Developing Library Human Resources*. Chicago: American Library Association, 1986.

- Be extremely knowledgeable about the subjects that they are teaching
- Relate well to people
- Be able teachers, and
- Be committed to attaining the goals of a training program.

Ideally, those who train should possess several personal attributes in addition to those listed above. These include an openness to different people and ideas, flexibility, enthusiasm for working with people, talent for judging employees' work performance, organizational skills, and a positive commitment to the library and to library work.

Librarians with training responsibilities will need to be evaluated by their superiors. Lists of the duties of the trainer and the expectations of training will need to be shared with any trainers. You will want to share the list of duties with the paraprofessional as well. A sample list of trainer duties and responsibilities is given in Figure 2-5.

After the training is planned and the trainer is selected, the library must begin the hiring process. The hiring process is outside the scope of this manual, but there are a number of useful resources available to help you. You will need to create a job advertisement, which can be done easily after you have written a job description, and you will need to conduct interviews. Based on the goals and objectives you have written you will be able to develop interview questions to determine what experience or interests the candidate has. Hiring can involve a great deal of paperwork including application forms or letters, communications with all applicants and those interviewed and other forms that may be required by your governing body. You should also be aware of a number of federal and state laws which govern the hiring process.

Planning is an essential component of the training process. Taking the time necessary to plan each aspect of training will help to ensure a thoughtful, well-developed training program. Careful planning will benefit the supervisor and trainer, the paraprofessionals, the reference department, and, ultimately, the library as a whole.

Figure 2-5

RESPONSIBILITIES OF A TRAINING COORDINATOR

1. Develop training aids, and utilize already developed aids, as appropriate (e.g. exercises, library guides).

2. Provide a tour of the library so that the Reference Assistants can successfully answer directional questions and lead tours.

3. Provide training in all forms of technology used in the library.

4. Hold meetings with the Reference Assistants to cover various aspects of reference work.

5. Explain or clarify the policies and procedures of the Reference Department.

6. Provide feedback on an individual basis.

7. Provide feedback on a group basis, usually in the form of written communication addressing a specific aspect of reference work or a specific problem noticed.

8. Provide periodic evaluation.

9. Schedule Reference Desk hours for Reference Assistants.

10. Coordinate and distribute special projects to the Reference Assistants and keep a record of these projects on a standard form noting the following items: nature of the project, date given, date completed, and any relevant comments.

11. Develop internal correspondence, as appropriate.

12. Provide any information needed for the Reference Assistants to function smoothly in the Reference Department.

13. Update and revise the training manual, preferably on an annual basis.

From Judith K. Ohles, *Training Coordinator's Manual: A Handbook for Training Preprofessionals at a Reference Desk.* Kent, OH: Kent State University. ERIC ED 301 221. 1988.

RESOURCES

Benson, Larry D. "Reference Assistant Training: An Integrated Approach." In *Enter, Save, Delete...: Libraries Pioneering Into the Next Century*, ed. by Douglas G. Birdsall, 16-43. Emporia, KS: Emporia State University, University Press, 1989. Benson discusses development of the training program for student reference assistants at Brigham Young University, and challenges of training students, setting objectives, and planning for evaluation and revision. Appendices include a training checklist and a training manual.

Bopp, Richard E., and Linda C. Smith, eds. *Reference and Information Services: An Introduction.* Englewood, CO: Libraries Unlimited, 1991. Bopp and Smith give a useful overview of reference service covering its history, philosophy, evaluation, management, and the use of reference interviews, search strategies, electronic resources, and training. They also describe specific reference sources.

Dewey, Barbara I. *Library Jobs: How to Fill Them, How to Find Them.* Phoenix: Oryx Press, 1987. Dewey provides advice about writing job descriptions, legal aspects of hiring, and job interviews.

Fontaine, France, and Paulette Bernhard for the General Information Programme and UNISIST. *Guidelines for Writing Learning Objectives in Librarianship, Information Science and Archives Administration.* Paris: UNESCO, 1988. Fontaine and Bernhard have created a step-by-step guide to writing training objectives, which includes worksheets to help trainers practice writing objectives.

Glogoff, Stuart, and James P. Flynn. "Developing a Systematic In-House Training Program for Integrated Library Systems." *College and Research Libraries* 48 (November 1987): 528-536. Glogoff and Flynn provide an introduction to adult learning theory while describing a training program at University of Delaware.

Guy, Jeniece. *Writing Library Job Descriptions*. Chicago: American Library Association, 1985. T.I.P. Kit 7. Reprints several articles from business and personnel journals that discuss why employers should write and how to write job descriptions. Also includes sample job descriptions from academic, public, and school libraries including both paraprofessional and professional positions.

Isenstein, Laura J. "Get Your Reference Staff on the STAR Track." *Library Journal* 117 (April 15, 1992): 34-37. Isenstein describes Baltimore County Public Library's training and peer coaching program, which has improved success in reference interviews.

Jones, Noragh, and Peter Jordan. "Staff Training and Development." Chapter 7 in *Staff Management in Library and Information Work*. Aldershot, Hants, England: Gower Publishing Company, 1987. Jones and Jordan give an extensive overview of methods and concerns related to training and staff development including identification of training needs, selection of training coordinator, resources, organization, and evaluation of training.

Rolstad, Gary O. "Training Adult Services Librarians." *RQ* 27 (Summer 1988): 474-477. Rolstad describes the three-part orientation program for new librarians offered by the Public Library of Columbus and Franklin County, Ohio.

Rubin, Richard E. *Human Resource Management in Libraries*. New York: Neal-Schuman Publishers, 1991. Rubin deals with all aspects of personnel including the hiring process.

Strubbe, Lisa Aren, and Diane G. Schwartz. "A Two-Year MLS Internship." *College and Research Libraries News* 49 (September 1988): 504-508. Strubbe and Schwartz discuss the training provided and objectives used by the Reference/Information Services Department at the Taubman Medical Library as well as an overview of the advantages for students and the department.

Woodard, Beth S. "Training, Development, and Continuing Education for the Reference Staff." In *Reference and Information Services: An Introduction.* ed. by Richard E. Bopp and Linda C. Smith, 151-170. Englewood, CO: Libraries Unlimited, 1991. Woodard provides an overview of planning for training with sections devoted to orientation, training, writing objectives and evaluation.

Woodard, Beth S., and Sharon J. Van Der Laan. "Training Preprofessionals for Reference Service." In *Reference Services Today: From Interview to Burnout*, ed. by Bill Katz and Ruth A. Fraley, 233-254. New York: The Haworth Press, 1987. Although intended to encourage libraries to use library science students at reference desks, Woodard and Van Der Laan provide an extensive overview of the management literature covering hiring, orienting, training, and evaluating.

3 TRAINING MANUALS

Chapter Overview

- Develop plan for manual
- Select materials to include
- Evaluate manual
- Revise manual

Library manuals are indispensable as training tools. Most commonly known as policy and procedure manuals, departmental manuals, or training manuals, they are mainly used to:

1. Assemble all related policies and procedures in one convenient form and place;
2. Maintain uniformity in staff actions;
3. Define departmental responsibilities, authority, and sometimes, hierarchy; and
4. Enable quick orientation of new employees by providing them with a basic understanding of the department and its activities.

A manual may also serve to reinforce what employees have learned in training sessions, place responsibility for learning the basic contents of the manual on the employee, indicate desired levels of performance, outline performance evaluation procedures, and provide a written reference to policies, procedures, and basic job skills for employees. If your library doesn't already have a manual (or several), you should consider developing one, both for training new employees and for everyday use.

This chapter will focus on the reference department instructional manual. Such a manual would be used to train new paraprofessionals and as a policy and procedure reference for the department. Covered will be development of a training manual, determining what to include, evaluation, and how to revise a manual.

DEVELOPING A MANUAL

One of the first important decisions to make is who will be responsible for developing a manual. The job can be assigned to a task force or committee, the managing supervisor with the input of all involved staff, or the supervisor alone. By appointing a task force or committee, the work is shared among different individuals. Several people can bring their ideas and input to the manual, and the writing style and content will more likely be appropriate

STAFF MANUALS

Manuals typically fall into four categories:

1. Inspirational: history, policy, and organization of the institution.
2. Regulatory: rules applying to all employees and patrons, such as hours, holidays, behavior, and privileges.
3. Informational: summary of scope and functions of all departments, giving information about each department which other departments should know.
4. Instructional: directions in detail for performing the various duties of departments or the duties of an individual.

From Frank W. Hoffman, "Procedure Manuals in Librarianship," in *Encyclopedia of Library and Information Science*, v.38, sup.3, 339-348. Allen Kent and Harold Lancour, eds. New York: Marcel Dekker, 1985.

for different levels of staff. In a smaller library, the supervisor may want to write or organize the manual.

Seeking staff input on manual development is advisable for several reasons. First, staff members may identify items to include that would otherwise be missed. Staff with specific responsibilities or experience can ensure that the parts of the manual covering these topics are written correctly. Second, asking for their input fosters a team spirit and makes it more likely they will use the manual. In short, involving staff will have a positive effect on department morale.

Another step in manual development is determining the objectives of the manual. The central question is: *What* should the manual do? There are three basic types of manuals based on purpose, although a manual may fulfill one or more of these purposes to varying degrees. Before writing a manual, you should decide which type or types your library needs. This decision will help provide the writers with guidelines for what to include. The three main objectives of manuals are:

1. **Training:** A *training* manual is intended to teach new staff how to function in the department. This may include specific directions for completing required tasks, a general orientation to the library or department, or a check list of areas for the new employee to become familiar with.

2. **Communicating:** A *communicating* manual is used to remind staff of all policies, and of seldom used procedures. It may also put into writing in a convenient place useful information about the library and its services such as library hours or circulation guidelines. The communicating manual tries to ensure that there is consistency among staff members in understanding policies.

3. **Administrating:** An *administrating* manual gathers all personnel policies for use by staff members and library administrators.

At this point, it may also be helpful to define policy and procedure so that staff clearly understand these concepts, and how to proceed to create a manual that addresses both. Policies generally provide guidelines that employees can follow in their work such as: It is our policy to provide prompt, accurate, courteous service to our users. A policy manual will include guides to the philosophy of the department. Policy statements should be expressed in positive language that is flexible and useful. Supervisors should use policy statements to put into writing the mission, philosophy, and understood policies of the library. Well-written policy statements will prevent misunderstandings, direct departmental employees towards the library's goals, provide support of employee decisions, and frame the answers to many questions posed by patrons.

Procedures, on the other hand, go through specific tasks step by step. They describe how an activity is performed, who is to perform the activity (when appropriate), and the chronology of the steps taken.

The format of the manual is another decision you will need to make. It should be based on the needs of the department and its employees. Factors to consider include the ease of referral and quick accessibility. Different arrangements of information include: from general to specific; alphabetical; most important first; or according to a classification scheme related to the purpose of the manual. If you think about how you expect the manual to be used you should see a logical organization. In general, policies probably belong in one section and procedures in another.

Another matter to resolve is how information is presented. Often, manuals use outline form; sections are defined and each piece of information about that subject is printed on a separate page. In this way, the manual can be easily updated by adding new pages or revising the text on any one page as needed. The one page per topic organization also encourages succinctness. Other formats that can be used include a narrative format, or flowcharts indicating preferred methods of following procedures.

WHAT TO INCLUDE?

The first step in the actual writing of a manual is gathering all information pertaining to departmental policies and procedures. You can adapt memos, reports, departmental documents, and materials from other departments (e.g., circulation policies, hours of branch libraries, etc.). Upon review of the documents, decide what will be included and excluded. Some of the documents may be changed before incorporating them into the manual.

If you plan to incorporate procedures, determine what should be included by observing staff at work, performing specific tasks yourself, or asking staff members to keep logs of their tasks and how they are accomplished. You may also want to review manuals from other libraries for ideas on possible formats and information to be included.

In general, you will want to include any information that affects the service you provide at the reference desk—policy statements such as:

- Circulation of reference materials
- Agreements with other libraries about referring patrons or questions
- Statement of confidentiality regarding patron inquiries
- Types or categories of patrons who are eligible for service
- Amount of time spent answering questions
- Use of specific resources (criss-cross directories or electronic sources, for example)

Successful manuals will clearly state the rationale for departmental policies and procedures. The *why* of these is important so that staff understand the background and reasons for doing tasks a specific way. With this understanding, staff are more likely to adhere to the policies and procedures that are stated in the manual.

More mundane information may be included as well. Consider incorporating useful items such as directions for:

- Adding paper or toner to copiers
- Unjamming printers
- Rebooting computers
- Logging on to different systems
- Downloading information from electronic resources
- Properly completing forms
- Reporting missing items
- Steps to follow when opening or closing the reference desk
- Playing messages left on the Reference Desk answering machine.

DO IT RIGHT

For maximum effectiveness, manuals need to:

- Be easy to read
- Be written in clear, concise language
- Be directed to the specific jobs and tasks of the department
- Include step-by-step directions
- Include a table of contents and an index

Gear the language of the manual to its readers. Simplify the steps included as much as possible to create a manual that is easily followed by all staff. It can be useful to think "If no reference staff member is in the library, what would a paraprofessional employee need to know to run this place?" This will cast the widest possible net for things to include, and from there you can eliminate the unimportant. If anyone in your library has ever taken time to write something down—whether formally in a policy statement, or more informally in a memo or set of directions left at the reference desk—then that bit of information is a candidate for inclusion in your manual. The ideal to strive for is a situation where any staff member with any question regarding reference service can be sure that "the answer is in the manual."

You can get ideas of what to include in your manual by reviewing other manuals. Ask your colleagues at other libraries to see or borrow a copy of theirs. The Standards Committee of the American Library Association's (ALA) Reference and Adult Services Division (RASD) has published an outline of a reference department manual. General sections that RASD recommends be included, as well as contents of other manuals, are listed in Figure 3-1. Subsets of each section can be found by consulting their complete outline. Outlines from three reference department manuals are shown in Figure 3-2.

Each department will need to gear its manual to its own needs. It is useful to include a table of contents and/or an index for easy access to specific items in the manual. Also include a blank page or two so that staff can quickly add notes or make suggestions for future revisions. A preface to the manual may indicate its purpose, and an introduction may state the mission of the reference department. These will set the tone for the rest of the manual. It may be useful to include the RASD Ethics of Service Statement:

- Information provided the user in response to any inquiry must be the most accurate possible. Type of question or status of user is not to be considered. Eligibility of users will be determined by the role, scope, and mission of individual institutions.
- Personal philosophies and attitudes should not be reflected in the execution of service or in the extent and accuracy of information provided.
- Information contacts with users, whether reference or directional, are to be treated with complete confidentiality.

Figure 3-1

RASD MANUAL OUTLINE

I.   Introduction
II.   Types of Service
III. Library Users
IV.   Priorities
V.   Desk Service Policies and Instruction
VI.   Interlibrary Loan Service
VII. Bibliographic Services
VIII. Information Correspondence
IX.   Document Services
X.   Orientation and Instruction Services

From American Library Association, Standards Committee, Reference and Adult Services Division, "A Commitment to Information Services: Developmental Guidelines," *RQ* 18 (Spring 1979): 277–278.

Figure 3-2

OTHER POSSIBLE MANUAL OUTLINES

1. Introduction

2. Objectives, goals, and activities

3. Organization

4. Reference Service

5. Resources

6. Branch library reference service

7. Evaluation and effectiveness of reference service

8. Forms

From Schippleck, Suzanne. *Library Reference Service*. Inglewood, CA: Inglewood Public Library, 1976.

Table of Contents

Introduction

1. Reference Desk Service, including:

  • Priorities

  • Handouts and Library Guides

- Assisting Users in Using Various Finding Aids
- Telephone Calls
- Amount of Service
- Referrals
- Complaints
- Directional Questions
- Repetitive Questions

2. Reference Desk Activities, including:

- Schedule
- Recording Statistics
- Activity During Slack Periods
- Opening/Closing the Reference Desk
- Maintenance of the Reference Area
- Approachability
- Emergencies

3. Other Functions of Reference

4. General Information (e.g. locations)

5. Commonly Asked Directional Questions and Their Answers

6. Student Assistants (i.e. special policies, instructions, and guidelines)

7. Appendixes

From Greg Byerly, Martha Goold, and Ruth Main. *Reference Training Manual*. Kent, OH: Kent State University, 1980.

Table of Contents

Preface

Introduction

1. Reference Desk Service to Users

2. Reference Desk Support Procedures

3. Off Desk Services of the Reference Department

4. Collection Development

5. Department Composition and Organization

6. Appendixes

From *Reference Policies and Procedures Manual*. Fairfax, VA: George Mason University, 1980.

• All rules and practices regarding availability and use of information or resources must be administered impartially. Rules and practices must be codified (i.e. reference policy statement) and made available to the user in written form.

• No personal financial gain should result because of the librarian/information specialist role as a representative of the Library in dealing with the user.

From *Reference Policies and Procedures Manual.* Fairfax, VA: George Mason University, 1980. (Adopted by the Reference and Adult Services Division Board, January 11, 1979). The RASD Ethics of Service Statement is reprinted with permission of the American Library Association.

EVALUATION

To determine a manual's effectiveness, it is advisable to evaluate it. One method of evaluation is to ask the reference staff for comments about the manual as they begin to use it. Have staff point out any redundancies, omissions, incorrect information, incomplete information, and confusing phrases they find. Another method is to observe staff using the written procedures in the manual. Compare what they actually do with what is written down to check for gaps in instructions. Staff can be asked to complete a questionnaire that specifically asks them to evaluate the effectiveness of the manual and identify particular problems, weaknesses, and strengths of the manual.

Finally, the manual can be tested by using it while training a new staff member. Determine if the staff member is learning what the manual sets out to teach, and if there are any noticeable gaps or errors in the instruction intended from the manual. If the new staff member is encouraged to use the manual, you will quickly become aware of what is not included in the manual. Also ask for feedback from the new staff member about the ease of use and accuracy of the manual.

REVISING

You never completely finish writing a manual. The writing of a manual is an ongoing process because it needs to be revised and updated on a regular basis. New policies, services, personnel, and major resources need to be reflected in the manual. With a manual that lists one policy or procedure per page, it is simple to make additions, deletions, or revisions. If you use this format, include a date somewhere on each page so that newly inserted material can be distinguished from other, older material. Revising a manual provides ideal opportunities to further test its effectiveness. Procedures can be reevaluated when changes occur in the library.

Every department needs to have an effective method for implementing revised or new procedures. The supervisor will also want some way to ensure that staff adhere to the revisions or additions stated in the manual. Good communication, staff input, and explanations for the new policies or procedures will ease their acceptance. It is also advisable to allow staff members to take an active role in revising the manual. A regularly revised manual will be a vital force in establishing guidelines and training staff.

A reference department manual is used for many purposes. Besides being an effective instrument for training new staff, it can establish guidelines for paraprofessionals to follow, gather policies and procedures in one place, encourage uniformity in staff actions, and provide criteria for amount and type of service provided. A manual is not a luxury; it is a must for the smooth functioning of a library department.

RESOURCES

American Library Association. Standards Committee, Reference and Adult Services Division. "A Commitment to Information Services: Developmental Guidelines." *RQ* 18 (Spring 1979): 275-278. The developmental guidelines for information services developed by RASD cover services, resources, environment, personnel, evaluation, and ethics. The appendix contains a sample outline of a reference services policy manual.

Carver, Deborah A. "Creating Effective Manuals: A Bibliographic Essay." *Library Administration and Management* 4 (Summer 1990): 145-148. Carver provides an overview of concepts important to writing user-friendly manuals and includes references to other sources of information.

Cubberley, Carol W. "Write Procedures That Work." *Library Journal* 116 (September 15, 1991): 42-45. Cubberley gives a practical guide to writing procedure statements or manuals that discusses writing, illustrations and typography.

Hoffman, Frank W. "Procedure Manuals in Librarianship." In *Encyclopedia of Library and Information Science*, ed. by Allen Kent and Harold Lancour, Volume 38 Supplement 3, 339-348. New York: M. Dekker, 1985. In addition to identifying the purposes, types, and contents of a procedure manual, Hoffman provides a review of the literature about procedure manuals and a list of manuals that might be consulted as examples.

Nichols, Margaret Irby. "The Reference Services Policy Manual." *Texas Library Journal* 63 (Spring 1987): 30-32. Nichols gives a thorough list of subjects to include in a department manual.

Ryan, Kathleen, and Peggy Royster. "The Procedure Manual." In *The How-To-Do-It Manual for Small Libraries*, ed. by Bill Katz, 132-140. New York: Neal-Schuman, 1988. Ryan and Royster offer step-by-step guidance for writing and revising a library procedure manual, including a definition of and reasons for having a procedure manual.

4 ORIENTATION

Chapter Overview

- Plan Orientation
- Prepare Orientation
- Discuss Personnel Procedures
- Give Orientation to Library
- Describe Service Philosophy
- Present Supervisor Expectations

Once a paraprofessional has been hired, he or she needs to be oriented to the library before actual training in job tasks begins. Employee orientation serves to welcome the new paraprofessional, provides information about the organization and the work, and builds a solid foundation for future training. During orientation, the supervisor will answer the who, what, where, when, how, and why of the many aspects of the library, the department, and the position. Successful orientation will:

- Decrease employee turnover;
- Enable the paraprofessional to be productive as soon as possible;
- Create feelings of satisfaction and enthusiasm in the paraprofessional; and
- Allow the paraprofessional to quickly feel like a part of the department.

This chapter will cover the various aspects of orientation including planning, initial preparation, the "housekeeping" duties necessary with new paraprofessionals, orientation sessions, and departmental introductions.

PLANNING ORIENTATION

In planning new employee orientation, you must consider all that the paraprofessional needs to know before, and soon after, he or she begins work. A training plan and a training calendar (sequence) will assist the supervisor in planning orientation activities. Another useful item is an orientation checklist. It should be as complete as possible to ensure that you do not forget anything that the paraprofessional needs to learn. A sample checklist is provided in Figure 4-1.

As the checklist is devised, you will need to decide who will handle each introduction or explanation. For example, the person responsible for the CD-ROMs may be the best person to give an introduction to them. You should also work out a timetable so that the paraprofessional will know what will happen during the first few weeks and so that other staff members who are involved in the orientation can arrange their schedules as needed.

Figure 4-1

TOPICS TO COVER IN ORIENTATION SESSIONS

Adapted from a handout developed by Marilyn Minney (Akron-Summit County Public Library) and Pamela Bradigan (Ohio State University Health Science Library), "Training and Orientation of a Newly Hired Reference Librarian." Ohio Library Association. Columbus, Ohio, October 1988.

Sample Checklist

I. INTRODUCTION TO PHYSICAL PLANT

Work Room   Reference Office
Work Stations   Floor Plans
Tour   Storage Areas
Supply Area   Book Collection
Meeting Rooms

II. LIBRARY OVERVIEW

Library organization chart   Department organization chart
Responsibilities of each staff member   Library long-range plans
Personnel evaluation   Departmental meetings
Department activities not
    related to reference desk
  Collection Development   Bibliographic Instruction
  Tenure and reappointment

III. PERSONNEL POLICIES AND PROCEDURES

Time clock/time sheet   Overtime
Lunch and breaks   Vacation time
Telephone use   Parking
Personnel Policy Manual   Probationary period
Communication with other staff
    (memos, meetings, bulletin board)
Staff development activities

IV. LOCATION OF COLLECTIONS

Ready Reference

Indexes

Special Collections

Easy Reading

Paperbacks

Electronic Products/Services

General Reference

Main Book Collection

Fiction

Large Print

Young Adult Materials

V. REFERENCE/INFORMATION DESK

Book donations

Vertical file

Pathfinders/Local bibliographies

Research process

Amount of time spent answering questions

Statistics form

Loaning supplies

Referral form

Typical patrons

Teaching vs. finding

VI. TELEPHONES

Etiquette

Taking messages

Personal calls

Basic answering

Transferring

Other features

VII. EQUIPMENT

CDROM

Microform printers and readers

Keys

Security system

Online searching

Elevator

Fire alarm

Copy machines

VIII. TEAMWORK APPROACH

Alertness to level of activity and
    need to assist coworkers

Expectations of supervisor

Sharing knowledge

  Materials

  Talents

Time spent away from desk

Open communication

Expertise

Resources

Procedure for closing the building

IX. PROBLEMS/COMPLAINTS

Patron behavior
    Rules   How to handle
    Backup from supervisor/colleagues
Complaints
    Library materials   Other
Cataloging
    Database errors   Spine label errors
Periodicals
    Missing issues   Missing pages

X. PUBLIC SERVICE POLICIES

Confidentiality of patron records   Library Bill of Rights
Public service philosophy   Guidelines about using electronic products
Interlibrary loan guidelines   Service at the Reference/Information Desk
Equal service to all   Initial contact with patrons
Legal and medical questions   Help with homework or contest questions

XI. EMERGENCIES

Calling Police or Fire Department, EMS   Flood
Tornado/Hurricane   Fire
Bomb threat   Gas leak
Closing of Library   Accidents
    Staff   Public
In charge of building procedures

XII. INTRODUCTION TO OTHER DEPARTMENTS/LIBRARIES

Introduction to Staff
Tours: All other departments
Tours: Local libraries to which patrons are referred

XIII. REFERENCE COLLECTION DEVELOPMENT

Choosing/ordering titles   Recommending titles
Learning to use new titles

INITIAL PREPARATION

The implementation of orientation begins between hiring the new paraprofessional and his or her first day of work. A welcoming letter, such as that found in Figure 4-2, should be sent to indicate the starting date; where, to whom, and at what time he or she should report; and any forms or documents he or she should bring (e.g., birth certificate or driver's license), if appropriate. You may also want to indicate in a letter what the paraprofessional can expect for the first few weeks, what work will be like at the beginning, and the aspects of orientation (Figure 4-2). You could also call the new paraprofessional several days before the starting date to confirm the first week's schedule and answer any last minute questions.

At the library, certain preparations should be made for the new employee's arrival. You should inform other staff members about the new paraprofessional, including starting date, background (e.g. former jobs, schooling), and the job description. The paraprofessional's work area should be readied. Have a copy of the departmental manual and the personnel manual ready for the paraprofessional, provide any supplies that will be needed, and make available any files relevant to the position.

"HOUSEKEEPING" DETAILS

The first few days of an employee's new job are crucial. You need to impart essential knowledge and make the new employee feel comfortable. The first few hours on the job should be devoted to welcoming the new employee into the department and taking care of necessary personnel procedures.

The paraprofessional will need to know specifics about the work environment and personnel policies. A personnel officer, if available, or the supervisor, should offer information about the institution, the department, and the specific job. Institutional items to be explained include paydays, payroll deductions, number and length of breaks, time clock or other time recording procedures, performance appraisal, organizational hierarchy, and personnel policies such as vacations, overtime, and sick leave. If a current staff manual is available, the new paraprofessional should be given a copy and a chance to review it and ask questions. Departmental items to cover include reference desk schedules, work practices, introductions to coworkers, department policies and procedures, what supplies are used and how to obtain them, and job responsibilities of each staff member. The

ORIENTATION DISCUSSION:

- Paydays
- Payroll deductions
- Breaks and lunches—how many and how long
- Procedures for recording hours worked
- Performance appraisal
- Organizational hierarchy
- Vacations, overtime, sick leave
- Current staff manual
- Other personnel policies

Figure 4-2

NEW EMPLOYEE WELCOME LETTERS

Dear _____,

   I am pleased to welcome you to the staff of _____ Library. As we discussed, you will be working as a Library Aide, twenty hours per week at the rate of $____ per hour.

   Mary Perkins, Library Aide Supervisor, will expect to meet you at the Reference Desk at 9:00 a.m. on Monday, March 18 to begin your four week training program.

   If I can be of any further assistance to you, please feel free to contact me at xxx-xxxx. I look forward to working with you.

Sincerely,

Director

Figure 4-2 Cont.

Dear _____,

I am very glad that you will be joining the Reference Department staff. Because I am your immediate supervisor, we will be working closely together. I look forward to getting to know you and developing a mutually rewarding work relationship.

Your first few weeks here are likely to be hectic ones. I will try to reduce any uncertainty you may feel by explaining some points of our training program.

1. When you arrive, you will receive a *Reference Department Training Manual*. Please read the manual thoroughly. We will have a meeting during the first week to go over the manual. I will also answer any questions.

2. The first and second weeks that you are scheduled at the Reference Desk, we ask that you not answer any questions. We have set aside this time so that you can observe the reference librarian to whom you have been assigned. As an observer, you will follow the professional librarians as they answer questions and respond to the requests of the patrons.

3. The third week that you are scheduled at the Reference Desk, we ask that you begin answering directional questions, but continue to observe librarians as they answer more indepth reference questions. By the fourth week, you may begin answering any questions with which you feel comfortable.

Again, I am looking forward to working with you. Please feel free to contact me with any questions or concerns, xxx-xxxx.

Respectfully yours,

Immediate Supervisor

Adapted from Judith K. Ohles, *Training Coordinator's Manual: A Handbook for Training Preprofessionals at a Reference Desk.* Kent, Ohio: Kent State University. ERIC ED 301 221. 1988.

DEPARTMENTAL ORIENTATION

- Reference desk schedules
- Work practices
- Introductions to coworkers
- Departmental policies and procedures
- Supplies and how to obtain them
- Job responsibilities of each departmental staff member
- Departmental manual
- Paraprofessional's job description
- Training schedule

paraprofessional should be given a departmental manual, and after reviewing it, the chance to ask questions concerning it. This is also the time to review the new paraprofessional's job description, answer any job-specific questions, and emphasize important aspects of the job.

It is also advisable to review the training that the paraprofessional will receive. Give the paraprofessional a schedule of the training and explain how training will proceed. You should talk about the observation time at the reference desk, explaining what the paraprofessional should expect and how to observe unobtrusively. Tell the paraprofessional that he or she will learn a great deal just by observing. It is helpful to offer suggestions about how to respond to patrons who ask the paraprofessional for help. Tell the paraprofessional how many weeks of observation are planned and when he or she should plan to begin trying to answer questions.

The initial period of orientation is also a time to get to know the employee better. It is helpful to meet frequently with the paraprofessional to begin the training process, answer any questions, get to know each other, and establish a good rapport. Sometimes an information sheet, such as the one in Figure 4-3, can succinctly provide information that was gathered in the interview process and make it more easily accessible. Information about interests and skills can not only make the getting acquainted process quicker, but can also serve as a reference for future projects or job duties.

ORIENTATION SESSIONS

Once the initial housekeeping details are in order, you can begin the more job-specific orientation sessions. These may include a tour of the library with a worksheet to assess any gaps in coverage, discussing the philosophy of the library and of reference service, and explaining standards and expectations, reference interviews, and reference search strategies. The last two will be discussed further in Chapter 5.

TOUR

A general tour of the library will enable the paraprofessional to begin answering directional questions at the reference desk. It is also important that paraprofessionals begin to know and under-

Figure 4-3

REFERENCE ASSISTANT INFORMATION SHEET

NAME _____

ADDRESS_____

_____

PHONE NUMBER_____

BIRTH DATE_____

MAJOR(S) AND MINOR(S) (high school or undergraduate)

_____

_____

OTHER AREAS OF INTEREST

_____

_____

SPECIAL SKILLS

_____

_____

Adapted from Judith K. Ohles, *Training Coordinator's Manual: A Handbook for Training Preprofessionals at a Reference Desk*. Kent, Ohio: Kent State University. ERIC ED 301 221. 1988.

stand their work environment. Therefore, a tour should be provided soon after the employee begins working, preferably on the first day of work. Try to avoid overwhelming the employee with details, but include all information that is immediately relevant to the paraprofessional's job. More detailed information will be provided in the departmental introductions.

It is helpful to have a written account of the areas covered on the tour so that the paraprofessional can refer back to it. Encourage the paraprofessional to add it to his or her training manual for easy reference. Writing out the tour also ensures that you will proceed through the library in a logical fashion and that you will remember all of the things you need to point out in a given area. It is very confusing for a new employee to be given a tour that returns to the same area three or four times because the tour guide suddenly remembers something he or she forgot.

Arrange the tour in some way that makes sense for the job. If patrons are given directions to an area that involves using an elevator, for example, have the tour go to that area and use the elevator. In this way the paraprofessional will be better prepared to give directions. The paraprofessional will be familiar with the elevator lobby as well as with directions for getting from the lobby to the desired destination. An example of a written library tour is provided in Figure 4-4.

Once the paraprofessional has had a tour of the library, it is useful to test his or her knowledge before permitting him or her to answer directional questions at the reference desk. This can also be a time to evaluate how well the employee understands some basic reference policies and procedures. A worksheet that includes items that the supervisor thinks are important can be an excellent tool in determining such basic understanding. Figure 4-5 is an example of such a worksheet based on the tour described in Figure 4-4.

The paraprofessional will also need to know what items are at the reference desk and work area. Again, a checklist of items will help the paraprofessional remember items in the area and can serve as a reference until the information is mastered (Figure 4-6).

DEPARTMENT INTRODUCTIONS

Department introductions are more thorough than library tours because they allow the staff of other library departments, sections, or branches to introduce the paraprofessional to the personnel, procedures, and resources of that area. You need to decide the best time during the training program to schedule department

Figure 4-4

A TYPICAL LIBRARY TOUR

BASEMENT

1. **FLIP (Freshmen Library Instruction Program) classroom.** Across from the Microform Center. FLIP provides freshmen students with a general orientation to the library. Students are given a lecture in the classroom, and are then given a tour of the first floor.

2. **Microform Center.** The Microform Center contains some current periodicals, some back issues on microfilm, and some current and back issues of newspapers. Patrons must first check the online catalog to determine if the library owns the desired item and where it is located. The Microform Center also contains ERIC (Educational Resources Information Center) documents, and microfilm and microfiche readers and printers.

3. **Restrooms.** Both men's and women's. Also located on the second and third floors near the elevator. On floors 4-10, men's are on even numbered floors, women's on odd numbered floors near elevators.

FIRST FLOOR

1. **Telephones.** Public pay phones are located on the first and third floors near the elevators. Campus/interlibrary phones are on floors 1-10 near the elevator (most are yellow).

2. **Photocopy machines.** Located on the first three floors in the elevator area.

3. **Circulation.** Near the exit. Patrons borrow and return books there as well as pay fines. To charge out materials, a library card is needed. Lost and found is located here.

4. **Reserves.** Attached to the circulation desk. A card catalog of reserve materials is located across from the reserves desk.

5. **Current periodicals.** Most current periodicals are shelved to the left of the escalator (coming into the building). They are shelved alphabetically, by title. The sorting range is located at the end of the stacks.

6. **Telephone books.** Books for the state are shelved separately, alphabetically by city. For the rest of the U.S., the books are on the remaining shelves, also alphabetically by city. Also some foreign telephone books. A card file in the Reference Center indicates which directories the library owns.

7. **Encyclopedias.**

8. **Reference collection.** Includes sources of general information—encyclopedias, atlases, almanacs, dictionaries, handbooks, and biographical directories. The sorting range for reference materials is located at the end of the stacks.

9. **Sorting range.** Books and periodicals are placed here before they are reshelved on the stacks.

10. **Card catalogs.** There are two card catalogs: Author/Title and Subject. The card catalog is not current (as of July 1987).

11. **Online catalog.** Located on every floor of the main library. Searchable by author, title, or subject to locate books, periodicals, government documents, and other library materials.

12. **Collections directory.** In the center of the card catalogs. It is a black sign-board with floor designations of books by call number. Copies of the Building Guide (at the Reference Desk) also indicate locations of materials.

13. **Library of Congress Subject Headings.** Red volumes between the card catalogs. Identifies appropriate subject entries for the online catalog and the subject card catalog.

14. **Index tables.** Contain frequently used indexes and abstracts. An alphabetical list is posted on columns near the consulting tables—gives table locations of indexes and abstracts.

15. **Reference desk.** Assistance is available most hours the library is open.

16. **Ready Reference Collection.** Materials frequently used by the reference staff are located here.

17. **Library guides.** Copies of library guides are available in the wooden rack in the lobby. They are specific to the library and provide good starting places for patrons to find material about certain topics.

Adapted from Judith K. Ohles. *Training Coordinator's Manual: A Handbook for Training Preprofessionals at a Reference Desk.* Kent, Ohio: Kent State University. ERIC ED 301 221. 1988.

Figure 4-5

LIBRARY TOUR WORKSHEET

Answer the following questions to the best of your ability. When the worksheet is completed, return it to me. Remember: this is not a quiz or a test, and will not be used in evaluations; this is simply a training device.

SHORT ANSWER

1. Where would one look to identify an appropriate subject heading for the online catalog or the subject card catalog?

2. What is the FLIP program?

3. The online catalog is searchable by:

4. Define sorting range:

5. One can determine the index table location of an index by:

6. Explain the usefulness of library guides:

MULTIPLE CHOICE

7. Microform Center houses:

   a. current periodicals

   b. back issues of periodicals

   c. microform readers and printers

   d. college catalog microfiche collection

   e. all of the above

Adapted from Judith K. Ohles, *Training Coordinator's Manual: A Handbook for Training Preprofessionals at a Reference Desk*. Kent, Ohio: Kent State University. ERIC ED 301 221. 1988.

Figure 4-6

LIST OF REFERENCE DESK ITEMS
Discussed During Orientation
1. Desk to Left of Reference Desk

- Procedures manual
- Ready Reference Manual—answers to often asked questions about the library
- Area phone directories

2. Reference Desk Counter

- Serials Catalog (red notebook), with lists of periodicals held at area libraries
- Reference Catalog (orange notebook)—list of sources in reference
- Emergency notebook
- Statistics sheet
- Library hours
- Log of notes from other reference staff
- Library of Congress Subject Headings
- Cash drawer and copy cards
- Form for charging cards
- Form for rejected cards

3. Shelf Behind Reference Desk

- Selected supplies
- Forms
- Handouts, including map of the library
- Road atlas

4. File Cabinet

- Supplies (top 2 drawers)
- Bibliographies, includes local information (third drawer)
- Maps and travel information (fourth drawer, front)
- Computer handouts and pamphlets (fourth drawer, back)

5. Ready Reference shelves

- New reference books
- Handouts
- Ready Reference books

visits. If the reference department refers many patrons to other departments, visits should occur early in the program, but if questions are rarely referred, department visits can wait until after the paraprofessional is comfortable with reference procedures and sources. There may be some departments the paraprofessional should visit soon after starting work and other departments that may not need to be visited until after the first month of training.

The purpose of the department introductions is to familiarize the paraprofessional with the personnel and activities of other sections in the library. These introductions should enable the paraprofessional to answer patron questions more effectively. After visiting the department and meeting the staff, the paraprofessional will be aware of where and to whom the patron is being referred. This can be important if the paraprofessional needs to give directions to the area or descriptions of employees to contact. If the paraprofessional visits a department that often refers patrons to reference, the paraprofessional will have a better understanding of what patrons encounter before they reach the reference desk.

Before contacting areas to be visited, you should review the questions most often referred by the reference department. For example, are patrons sent to the main library? Are they referred to the government documents staff? Is it often suggested that patrons use the children's collection? Are patrons often redirected to the reserve desk when they mistakenly believe they have been sent for a book in reference? Also review questions other departments receive from reference. Is technical services consulted to see if an item has been ordered, received, or processed? Is circulation called to see if a book is available? If so, all of these areas are places to which the reference paraprofessional should be introduced by a supervisor from that department. Also consider questions that are often referred to reference. Does the government documents department refer patrons to the reference area to use the *Monthly Catalog*? Are patrons sent from the periodical collection to the indexes located in or near the reference area?

After deciding which departments of the library should be visited, the supervisor should think about what the paraprofessional needs to learn while in each section. Following are some questions to consider:

When is this department staffed? This is especially important if the department is not staffed during the same hours that reference is staffed. The paraprofessional should be made aware that the department may be closed when reference is open and informed about whether the public still has access to the materials kept there.

Who works in this department? To make referral easier, the paraprofessional should know the names of the employees in other departments. This is also helpful because it increases the visibility of the reference staff and introduces the paraprofessional to other members of the library staff. If patrons approach the reference desk in search of particular library employees, the paraprofessional can correctly direct the patron to the correct location or department.

What is done in this department? The paraprofessional needs to know what is done in other areas of the library. This information is useful for answering patron questions. For example, after learning who processes donated books, the paraprofessional will know to whom questions about book donations should be referred.

What is the work flow in this department? It will be helpful for the paraprofessional to understand how work moves through the library. What happens to a book once it is received by the library? What departments does it have to go through before it is available to the public? Can the process be speeded up at any point if a patron in the building wants the book immediately? If the paraprofessional is familiar with the work flow, personnel, and policies of other library departments, he or she will know what steps to take when answering patron questions that concern activities of other library departments.

What materials should reference department personnel know about? Some reference sources may not be kept in the reference section where the paraprofessional works. For example, the *Monthly Catalog* may be kept in government documents; or *Something About the Author* may be in the children's department. If the reference department often refers patrons to sources that are not in the reference collection, the paraprofessional should be told where those sources are kept. Use and coverage of the sources should be explained to the paraprofessional so that he or she can confidently refer patrons to the sources when necessary.

Which patrons and questions should be referred to this department? If there are questions that are always referred to this department, the paraprofessional should be made aware of the questions and told why this department answers them. Is all of the library's material about patents kept in government documents? Are all of the nursery rhymes and fable books in the children's collection? Are all of the monies collected at the business office?

Which patrons and questions should not be referred to this department? There may be patrons who should not be referred to a specific department. For example, if the video collection contains only educational videos, the paraprofessional should not refer patrons in search of recent box office hits to the video department. The most recent issues of some newspapers or magazines may be on reserve rather than in the periodical collection. Make sure the paraprofessional is aware of exceptions.

Should reference staff members call before sending a patron to this department? If the department wants reference staff to call before sending patrons to its area, this should be explained to the paraprofessional during the visit to the department.

Which patrons and questions does this department refer to reference? The paraprofessional needs to recognize that patrons may have been to several departments before they arrive at reference. This may frustrate patrons, and the paraprofessional should be alerted to this problem.

Does this department call before referring patrons to reference? If reference is called, the paraprofessional should be told how these phone calls are to be handled. Is a reference staff member expected to find an answer while the patron is traveling to reference? Will the patron simply be referred to the reference desk or sent directly to the staff member who took the call?

Once it is known what must be covered in the department visits, you should contact the head of the department that will be visited first. You will need to explain the purpose of the training and ask if the supervisor or another staff member could spend some time giving the paraprofessional a tour of the department and discussing the items identified as important. Also see if the department head has suggestions for other information the paraprofessional might need. The presenter may need to prepare handouts to further explain what he or she will be discussing. These handouts can include names and phone numbers of members of the department when appropriate, and may be added to the paraprofessionals' training manual for future use.

Be sure to schedule the department visit during a time that will be convenient for the reference desk, the paraprofessional, and the department to be visited. You should tell the paraprofessional when and where the session will be, who the paraprofessional will meet, and what the topic will be.

Some of the items discussed in the department visit may be a repeat of information the paraprofessional received at other points in the training program or work experience. This will reinforce the information for the paraprofessional. It is possible that the department personnel will be able to explain departmental policies or procedures to the paraprofessional, and this information could be useful in explaining some situations to patrons. For instance, reference department staff might not understand why it takes three days to get a magazine from the mailroom to the public shelves, but a visit to the serials processing area would probably explain why this occurs.

Ideally, you as the trainer or supervisor will attend the department visits with the paraprofessional. This will allow you to point out connections to the reference department as well as prepare you for any follow-up questions that might occur. You will also have an opportunity to prompt the presenter if you think he or she has not mentioned something that the paraprofessional needs to know.

After the department introduction, you should take a moment to reflect on the session yourself, perhaps making notes for future use. Are there things the presenter should have included? Note these items so that the next time the department is visited, you can request that these points be covered. You might realize that a change could be made in all of the department visits. The paraprofessional should also be asked for comments on the visits and the presentations and for questions about the material covered. Finally, a thank you note should be sent to the presenter, with a copy sent to the presenter's supervisor.

HELPFUL SOURCES

Encourage new paraprofessionals to be aware of resources that apply to or guide library service, such as:

- Library Bill of Rights
- RASD Ethics of Service Statement (see p. 35)
- Statement of Professional Ethics
- Guidelines for Medical, Legal and Business Responses at General Reference Desks
- *Intellectual Freedom Manual*

PHILOSOPHY OF SERVICE

It is vitally important to include attitudinal training early in the orientation process. Reference paraprofessionals need to learn how to deal with the public effectively in order to become successful at reference work. Early orientation to the public service philosophy of the library can prevent future problems in dealing with patrons. One way to begin attitudinal training is for you to discuss your philosophy of public service with the paraprofessional. You will want to get the paraprofessional to think about public service philosophy and discuss what he or she believes the library's philosophy of service is. This should be done early in orientation so that any problems or misunderstandings can be addressed. For example, a library's philosophy of service may be to instruct patrons in the use of sources so that patrons can become more self-sufficient in using the library. This needs to be communicated to the paraprofessional.

You may want to begin a discussion of service philosophy with a case study related to public service, a role-playing session followed by a discussion, or by simply asking the new employee for a definition of public service. Several sample situations for use in starting case studies or role plays follow. These situations are brief so that you can use them as case studies or role-plays. With this brief introduction, you can write a fuller description of the situation using references to real locations or collections in your building as well as references to policies and procedures used at your library. The "right" answer to these situations will depend on the philosophy and policies followed by each library.

Case 1: You have helped two different patrons who have a great deal of interest in photography. One is interested in starting her own studio and the other is interested in the technical aspects of photography and wants to start his own business. In helping both of them find information related to their goals, you believe they may be able to help each other. Can you introduce the two? Can you tell either of them about the interests of the other? Should you just hope they will someday meet in the photography section of the library?

Case 2: While you help a patron locate copies of last year's *Newsweek*, you see a teenager quickly put something in his pocket that you believe is a knife, shove a volume back on the shelf and leave the periodicals area in a hurry. When you look at the volume, you see that several pages have been removed. When you return to the front lobby of the library, you see the teenager leaving the library. What should you do?

Case 3: An obviously angry patron approaches the reference desk. He says, "The stupid girl at the circulation desk will not let me borrow this book. She says the computer says I have two expensive art books three weeks overdue. I don't like art. I've never checked an art book out of any library let alone this rinky-dink little place. You tell her I pay my taxes and I am allowed to borrow this book no matter what that blankety-blank computer says!" How do you respond?

Case 4: An older gentleman, who has been using the online catalog, asks you to assist him. He points to the record on the screen for the book called *Final Exit*. He asks why his tax dollars are being spent to provide this kind of "anti-Christian garbage". Another lady, who is standing nearby, breaks in to tell you she agrees with the first gentleman. What should you do?

Case 5: A patron with a thick accent asks you a reference question. You have asked her to repeat the question several times but still cannot understand what she needs. How can you proceed?

Case 6: A young woman wearing a swastika on her shirt approaches the reference desk and asks you for directions for making a bomb. How do you react? What if the patron is wearing a suit and tie?

Case 7: You help a student with a rather difficult research paper topic—the effect of second hand cigarette smoke on household pets. Using several indexes available in the library, you identify a few articles about the subject which appeared in magazines that the library does not own. The student writes down the citations, thanks you for your help and leaves the library. Several weeks later, a teacher approaches the desk and tells you that she believes one of her students plagiarized his paper about the effect of second hand smoke on household pets. The teacher would like your help finding information about this topic so that she can compare the writing of the student with that of previously published sources. What should you do? Can you find out if it was the same student?

How does your response change if your library owns the magazines the student used?

Case 8: Every evening that you work at the Reference Desk, Mrs. Smith, a recent widow, comes to the library and begins talking to you. She always begins by asking a reference question—sometimes about a recipe she wants, or the words to a poem she vaguely remembers or the address of a company to which she wants to write. After getting you to the stacks to help her find the requested information, she begins talking about her husband. This usually leads to tears and keeps you occupied for a least ten minutes and usually longer. Other patrons are waiting while you try to console Mrs. Smith and answer her original question, in which she is rarely interested after she has asked it. What should you do? What can you do in the future when she approaches the desk?

In any discussion of service philosophy, you may want the following points to be discussed:

1. The patron is our first priority.
2. Courtesy and a helpful attitude should be used at all times.
3. Be approachable.
4. Listen carefully to all of the patron's request.
5. Try to put the patron at ease throughout the entire reference transaction.
6. Keep the patron informed about what you are doing to answer his or her question, and do not make patrons wait for extended periods of time.
7. If you cannot answer the question, admit this to the patron and suggest what other action can be taken.
8. It is acceptable to refer questions to other staff, and it is better to do this than give a wrong or incomplete answer.
9. All patrons should be treated the same in accordance with library policies.
10. Patrons with concerns or complaints should be taken to private areas and perhaps be referred to a supervisor or department manager.

SERVING PATRONS

Explain how your library is funded. Point out that tax paying citizens or tuition paying students fund the purchase of materials and the salaries of personnel available in the library. They have paid for service that meets their needs and deserve to receive the best possible service every employee can provide.

Because a public service philosophy is vital to providing good reference service, it is important to periodically re-emphasize the philosophy. The memo in Figure 4-7 is ideal to use shortly after the new employee has been hired; the memo in Figure 4-8 can be used as a follow-up two to three months after the paraprofessional has begun work.

It is also important to discuss library policies regarding library service with the paraprofessional. How much time is typically spent with each patron? Are patrons taught to use sources or are paraprofessionals expected to find the needed answers? Should the amount of service given depend on the purpose of the questions (homework, trivia, crossword puzzles, contests)? Are there charges for any services (e.g., online searches, interlibrary loan, holds, or recalls)? Are in-person and phone patrons given the same priority or the same level of service? How are patrons referred to other libraries? How are questions referred to other librarians?

It is useful to talk to the paraprofessional about your library's typical patrons. Identify common social, economic, or educational backgrounds. If you have a group of patrons resistant to your online catalog or other electronic resources, they should be identified for the paraprofessional and strategies for working with them should be discussed. Point out how the clientele changes with time of day or time of year.

Another important aspect of public service is learning how to deal with problem patrons. Paraprofessionals should be trained in this so that they will feel relatively comfortable with any situation that may arise. Good orientation techniques for dealing with problem patrons include role-playing and discussion, and case studies. A written reminder, such as the one in Figure 4-9, can also be helpful for the paraprofessional.

STANDARDS AND EXPECTATIONS

Each library, and each supervisor, has standards of work performance and expectations of the library staff. It is your responsibility, as supervisor, to let employees know that behavior and work performance are important to you. Paraprofessionals will be more productive and will feel more secure in their jobs if they

Figure 4-7

PHILOSOPHY OF SERVICE MEMO: I

TO: Reference Assistants

SUBJECT: ELEMENTS FOR PROVIDING IDEAL REFERENCE SERVICE

We are glad to have you join the reference staff and hope your first few weeks here have been ones of learning, growth, and enjoyment. You are now a member of our team and will help in our efforts to provide our patrons with courteous, efficient, and effective reference service. Following are some guidelines to keep in mind to help you provide the best possible service to our patrons. As always, please let me know if I can be of any assistance.

Guidelines

1. Treat patrons with politeness and friendliness. Many are intimidated by the library, and a friendly face helps relieve some of their fears and anxieties. We are here not just to provide information, but to make people feel comfortable with the library. Also, good, efficient, and friendly service is our best form of PR.

2. You may notice some patrons coming up to the desk timidly, saying that they have "a stupid question." My pat answer to that is "There's no such thing." Many people have very little experience with libraries, and some of their biggest fears are that they don't know something that they should, that everyone else knows how to use the library, and that people will think they are stupid. We can do much to alleviate these fears by treating each patron and each question with respect.

3. Escort patrons to sources and instruct them in the use of sources. Give thorough explanations. This will ensure that patrons know how to use sources correctly, and will also make them feel comfortable coming back to the reference desk the next time they need assistance. At least, ask patrons if they have used a specific source before. Before leaving patrons, invite them to come back to the desk if more information is needed.

4. Give patrons options. Often patrons are frustrated when they can't find what they need and suggesting other possible sources can alleviate their frustration. For example, if a book a patron wants is not on the shelf, suggest using the online catalog (instruct in use of the catalog if the patron has not

used it before) to see if the library carries the book. Also suggest that the patron place a hold on the book. Finally, suggest that the patron check with area libraries. We can also suggest Interlibrary Loan as an option.

5. Give each patron the time and attention that he or she needs. Make sure the patron understands your directions/instructions before going back to what you were doing at the desk. Make sure you've answered his or her question(s) thoroughly. Patrons are our first priority, and should be treated as such.

6. Look around frequently to become aware of people who may need assistance and are timid about coming up to the desk to ask for your help. Looking up from work being done at the desk also lets patrons know that we are not too immersed in our own work or activities to help them. We want to avoid being engrossed in library work or reading while at the reference desk—this gives patrons the wrong impression that we are interested in other things, rather than in helping them.

Again, don't hesitate to contact me with any questions or concerns. You're doing well and have made a fine start. Thanks for your efforts!

Figure 4-8

PHILOSOPHY OF SERVICE MEMO: II

TO: Reference Assistants

SUBJECT: ELEMENTS FOR PROVIDING IDEAL REFERENCE SERVICE 2

Following are more "ideal qualities of reference staff" lists. These lists describe the kind of high quality reference service for which we strive. To improve our work performance at the reference desk, we may want to use the following as "checklists" in our daily work. Certainly we cannot attain all of these qualities immediately. However, if we work on even just one each week, we will continually improve service to our patrons.

QUALITIES ASSOCIATED WITH GOOD REFERENCE SERVICE
A. Behavioral Characteristics/Attitude and Demeanor
Approachability
Sense of willingness

Attitude—friendly—not condescending or didactic

Ability to communicate

Acknowledgment of patrons who are waiting

Determination to do a good job

Ability to effectively deal with problem personalities

Positive response/attitude towards questions

Alertness to patrons needing help but not asking for it

Nonjudgmental responses

Positive responses to unusual questions

B. Knowledge of

Resources and collections

Alternative sources

When to refer

Subject

Correct use of reference tools

Library services and policies

C. Reference Skills

Thorough investigation of a problem

Provision of search strategy to patron

Systematic approach

Awareness of not knowing the answer, and when to refer

Development of methodology for answering "unanswerable" questions

Clear, logical thinking

Ability to use all resources available

Ability to buy time when you need it

Investigative knowhow

Knowledge of our resource and time limitations

Effectiveness in interviewing: gets to the user's real question

Ability to provide assistance at patron's level of need

Ability to teach patrons how to use resources

Reprinted with permission. Diane G. Schwartz and Dottie Eakin, "Reference Service Standards, Performance Criteria, and Evaluation," *Journal of Academic Librarianship* 12 (March 1986): 5.

Figure 4-9

PROBLEM PATRONS MEMO

TO: Reference Assistants

SUBJECT: Problem Patrons

We sometimes come across patrons who are frustrated and may take their frustrations out on those of us behind the reference desk who cannot meet all of their needs or expectations. Some points crucial to handling any "problem patron."

Acknowledge what you can or cannot do with the given circumstances. You cannot and are not expected to be a policeman or a counselor.

You will appear vulnerable and weak if your response or attitude change during an exchange. Be consistent.

Be flexible, finding other avenues to meet the patron's need.

Use "we" rather than "I". This gives the impression that you are carrying out library policy and are not picking on this particular person on your own.

Be assertive, honest, and direct without becoming aggressive, insulting, or hostile. Be aware of your tone of voice and try to always maintain a friendly tone.

If you suspect a personality conflict, have another staff member intervene (e.g., the supervisor).

A final note: remember that you are not alone in feeling frustrated or angry with patrons. The difficult lesson for all of us to learn is how to feel frustrated without showing it.

THANKS!

YOUR SUPERVISOR'S EXPECTATIONS OF EMPLOYEES

1. Keep an open mind and a positive attitude.
2. Remain self disciplined.
3. Take initiative in your work.
4. Think through problems and identify possible alternative solutions.
5. Extend courtesy by keeping me informed of what you are doing and if you are stuck.
6. Talk with me when you need to.
7. Confront me with problems that you have because of me.
8. Maintain the best image possible with other staff members, patrons, and library / community / organization / university leaders.
9. Foster a sense of teamwork.
10. Celebrate the different backgrounds, styles, values, and ideas of others.
11. Maintain professional integrity.
12. Be yourself.

From a handout developed by Aldis M. Knight, "How To Establish Standards and Expectations." Supervisory Skills Series, Career Development/Personnel Services, Purdue University, West Lafayette, Indiana, 1989. Mr. Knight is the Director of Staff Training and Development at Purdue University.

understand what is expected of them. Therefore, you will want to be honest and forthright in identifying organizational standards with them. These items are sometimes covered in a staff manual and are usually covered in the items that are included in a performance evaluation.

Each supervisor will want to establish his or her own expectations of, as well as obligations to, employees. You may want to schedule a meeting with new staff to discuss these expectations, ensure that they are understood, and clear up any possible concerns or misunderstandings. You may wish to give written copies of your expectations to paraprofessionals to include in their training manuals.

It is helpful to explain the performance evaluation procedures to new employees during the orientation process. Give them a copy of their evaluation form and discuss satisfactory and unsatisfactory performance in each category. For example, in the area of promptness, you might point out that arriving five minutes early is satisfactory but that arriving more than five minutes late more than once each month is unacceptable.

Proper orientation and further training can only benefit the library and the patrons being served. It is essential to spend time creating a successful orientation program to get new employees off to a good start. The beginning days and weeks of a paraprofessional's employment is vital to their learning the proper skills, being effective at their jobs, and having a good attitude about the library and their work. A well-developed orientation program will ensure that they become fully functioning members of the reference department as quickly as possible.

RESOURCES

Berwind, Anne May. "Orientation for the Reference Desk." *RSR: Reference Services Review* 19 (1991): 51-54, 70. Berwind presents the five practical steps for orientation: service philosophy, reference desk transactions, tours, procedures, and reference sources.

Bloomberg, Marty. "Reference Services." In *Introduction to Public Services for Library Technicians*, ed. by Marty Bloomberg, 67-76. Littleton, CO: Libraries Unlimited, 1985. Bloomberg discusses how to prepare Library Media

YOUR SUPERVISOR'S OBLIGATIONS TO EMPLOYEES

1. Communicate information that affects your jobs.
2. Be fair and consistent in evaluation of your performance.
3. Meet regularly.
4. Provide informal/formal feedback as a routine.
5. Be honest.
6. Be open for ideas.
7. Listen to ideas and consider them.
8. Champion your good ideas and act upon them whenever possible.
9. Give credit where due.
10. Train/develop where needed.
11. Reward/guide/direct/challenge with purpose of obtaining appropriate results.
12. Correct inappropriate behavior.

From Aldis M. Knight, "How To Establish Standards and Expectations." Supervisory Skills Series, Career Development / Personnel Services, Purdue University, West Lafayette, Indiana, 1989. Handout. Mr. Knight is Director of Staff Training and Development at Purdue University.

Technical Assistants for reference work, reviews how to deal with patrons and how to analyze questions, explains the organization of reference collections, and discusses the limits on reference services employed by some libraries.

Flinner, Beatrice E. "A Scenario of the Reference Librarian in a Small University Library." *The Reference Librarian* 19 (1987): 341-358. Flinner gives an overview of what a reference staff member encounters on the job including professionalism, reference interview, patrons, communication, policy manuals, responsibilities, technology, education, evaluation and collection development.

Kathman, Michael D., and Jane M. Kathman. "Integrating Student Employees into the Management Structure of Academic Libraries." *Catholic Library World* 56 (March 1985): 328-331. Kathman and Kathman discuss the selection, training, and supervision of students employed in academic libraries. They stress the importance of using the selection and training stages to acquaint the student with library goals and enable them to see how their work helps the library meet its goals.

Loraine, Kaye. "Taking the Pain Out of Orientation." *Supervision* 50 (May 1988): 3-5. Loraine emphasizes the feelings of a new employee and reminds supervisors to provide as much orientation and nurturing as the employee needs. She recommends "streamlining" orientation to avoid immediately overwhelming new employees with minute and possibly less important details.

Luccock, Graham. "Induction Training." In *Handbook of Library Training Practice*, edited by Ray Prytherch, 3-36. Aldershot, Hants, England: Gower, 1986. Luccock discusses why orientation is important and how to plan for an orientation program including: selection of orienters, determination of what orientation is needed, selection of orientation methods, and evaluation of an orientation program.

McMurry, Nan. "From Library Student to Library Professional: Smoothing the Transition for the New Librarian." *North Carolina Libraries* 49 (Winter 1988): 209-213. While intended for new professional librarians and their supervisors, McMurry reminds both reference desk staff and supervisors about dealing with uncertainties and orientation for new reference desk employees. She discusses knowledge of the library and the collection, the reference interview, mentoring, and informal communication networks.

"Off to a Good Start: A Checklist for the Training of the New Librarian." *Ohio Libraries* 3 (January/February 1990): 6-7. A thorough list of topics to cover during orientation including personnel matters, library and department overviews, and individual responsibilities.

5 REFERENCE INTERVIEW

To answer reference questions successfully, it is important that paraprofessionals learn how to handle the reference interview. The purpose of the reference interview is to find out exactly what the patron wants.

An ideal reference interview occurs when a patron asks for reference assistance and the library staff member, through dialogue with the patron, determines the information needs of the patron and interprets the question and subsequent answer in terms of the library's resources.

This negotiation for information must take place before attempting to answer the patron's reference question. If the library staff member does not determine the exact nature of the patron's request, the patron may receive misinformation, the library staff member and the patron may waste valuable time looking for unneeded or inappropriate information, and the patron may experience undue frustration with the library. For these reasons, reference interviewing is a vital skill for all reference staff.

This chapter will cover methods of teaching the reference interview, preparing for the reference interview, reference interview strategies, specific communication problems, reference search strategies, and closing the reference interview.

METHODS OF TEACHING

There are several different methods of teaching paraprofessionals how to negotiate the reference interview. Some of the methods include holding a workshop, role playing, routing articles followed by a discussion period, and observing other staff members.

A workshop is a particularly useful way to introduce paraprofessionals to the concept and philosophy of the reference interview. Here you can:

- Define "reference interview" (see Figure 5-1).
- Indicate the necessity for the reference interview
- Describe successful reference interviewing techniques
- Discuss important nonverbal clues
- Point out potential problems in reference interviews

Figure 5-1

REFERENCE INTERVIEW DESCRIPTIONS

The reference interview is "one of the most complex acts of human communication because one person tries to describe for another person not something he knows, but rather something he does not know."

Karen M. Moss. "The Reference Communication Process." *Law Library Journal* 72 (Winter 1979) 48–52.

William A. Katz believes a reference interview is a "dialogue between someone in need of information and someone—the librarian—able to give assistance in finding it."

Introduction to Reference Work volume 2 *Reference Service and Reference Processes.* 4th ed. NY: McGraw-Hill, 1982.

Laura Isenstien defines "the reference interview as a complex communication process between two human beings, where the librarian must facilitate communication that encourages the patron to describe what it is [he or she] needs to know."

"On the Road to STARdom." *Illinois Libraries* 73 (February 1991): 146–151.

"The seed of the answer is with the question, and librarians play a special role— empathetic communication, knowledge of information sources and how to access them, and the ability to teach users some of the information searching procedure."

Anne Page Mosby, and Glenda Hughes. "Continuing Education for Librarians—Training for Online Searching." *The Reference Librarian* 30 (1990): 105–118.

"As long as patrons continue to ask broad, indefinite questions, reference librarians will have the responsibility to use proven negotiation techniques that lead to the real information need."

Thomas Ricks, et al. "Finding the Real Information Need: An Evaluation of Reference Negotiation Skills." *Public Libraries* 30 (May/June 1991): 159–164.

Rochelle Yates writes, "Any familiarity with the reference interview teaches us that while the patron starts out with *a* question, it may not necessarily be *the* question. That progression from an incomplete or vague statement to the patron's true need is critical, if we are to arrive at a usable answer."

A Librarian's Guide to Telephone Reference Service. Camden, CT: Library Professional Publications, 1986.

- Identify different questions that may be asked
- Identify the types of sources most useful in answering reference questions

USING VIDEOS

It may be useful to use videos from the Library Video Network (LVN) to help paraprofessionals understand the importance of the reference interview and develop effective service attitudes. LVN is a project that grew out of the cooperation of twelve library systems in Maryland. When the systems recognized that they had common training needs, they joined forces to develop training programs such as:

If It Weren't For the Patron, which stresses the importance of public service attitudes, and *Who's First . . . You're Next,* which describes methods of handling a busy reference desk. A program focusing on special patrons is featured in *Sensitivity to the Disabled Patron.*

It is important to ensure that the workshop really is a workshop, and not merely a lecture or presentation. A workshop is of very limited value if you do all of the talking. It is important to involve the paraprofessional in discussions of interviews he or she has observed at the reference desk, to ask the paraprofessional to engage in role plays with you to demonstrate good and bad reference interview behaviors, and to practice using the best techniques.

With role playing, you can play the patron and demonstrate the possible problems that can occur during the reference interview. This method will also show the paraprofessional how vital it is to learn effective reference interviewing techniques. A good trainer will be able to reflect the many variations of patron communication, including hesitancy to ask a question, embarrassment at not knowing how to use the library, unsophisticated communication skills, and vague questions. You can also pretend to be a librarian and demonstrate how not to conduct a reference interview. At first, you may need to tell the paraprofessional what the initial question should be and what he or she "really" wants to know when pretending to be the patron. Following are several problem reference interview questions which you can use to begin role plays:

Question: Where are the nutrition journals?

Need: Information about latest fad diet

Question: Where are your family law books?

Need: Brother sold me a stereo and now he won't let me have it

Question: Do you have an atlas?

Need: Distance between Atlanta and Washington, D.C.

Question: Is all of your information in this computer?

Need: Statistics about mortality rates in Africa

Question: Where are books about Nixon?

Need: Text of Checker's Speech

Question: Do you have French music here?

Need: Words to national anthem of France

Question: What is "tree" and "root"?

Need: Definitions of computer terms

Question: I need dictionaries of Native American languages

Need: States whose names come from Indian terms

Question: Why are these books in the rest room?

Need: Misunderstood call number "RR"

HELPFUL SOURCES

There are a number of sources you might have the paraprofessional read, including:

Christopher W. Nolan. "Closing the Reference Interview: Implications for Policy and Practice." *RQ* 31 (Summer 1992): 513–523.

Mary Goulding. "Real Librarians Don't Play 'Jeopardy'." *Illinois Libraries* 3 (February 1991): 140–146.

Catherine Sheldrick Ross, and Patricia Dewdney. Chap. "Interviewing" in *Communicating Professionally*. New York: Neal-Schuman Publishers, 1989.

Elaine Zaremba Jennerich, and Edward J. Jennerich. *The Reference Interview as a Creative Art*. Littleton, CO: Libraries Unlimited, 1987.

Routing articles about the reference interview can be an effective method of reinforcing previous training. This will remind the paraprofessional of the importance of reference interviewing and its various methods. You may want to hold a discussion about the articles to get feedback from the paraprofessional, answer any questions he or she may have, clear up any possible misunderstandings, and emphasize especially relevant points. This method is useful as a reminder and review of training.

Observation is a good technique for learning reference interview skills. When possible, the paraprofessional should observe several different librarians. This way he or she can observe different styles of interviewing, and determine which method or methods is most effective or suitable. It is also helpful if the librarian, after the exchange with the patron has taken place, explains his or her method of interviewing and describes how he or she decided on the specific sources to recommend.

It is useful to ask the paraprofessional to take notes about particularly difficult or confusing questions that are observed at the reference desk. These sample requests can be used in later discussions or training sessions. You might suggest the paraprofessional take notes along these lines:

1. Question as first stated by patron
2. Librarian's interpretation of question
3. Real question of patron

For example, a patron may ask for books about Abraham Lincoln but really want to know who gave the speech after Lincoln's Gettysburg Address. Or a patron might ask for the Pope's address and be surprised by a mailing address rather than a speech text. As the paraprofessional observes and records troublesome questions, he or she will become aware of the difficulties surrounding the reference interview.

PREPARING FOR THE INTERVIEW

Paraprofessionals should be encouraged to "invite" reference questions. This involves appearing approachable and when necessary (according to library policy), approaching patrons who appear to have questions. Tell the paraprofessional that appearing approachable involves a number of nonverbal behaviors and environmental considerations. Encourage the paraprofessional to keep the reference desk area clutter-free. When finished using reference materials, they should be removed from the reference desk so that patrons will not have to approach a person buried behind a wall of books.

The paraprofessional should avoid waiting on hold for long periods of time. When waiting for an answer which will take more than a few minutes, the paraprofessional should ask the person he or she called to return the call when the answer is found. In this way, the paraprofessional remains free to help other patrons.

You will need to talk to the paraprofessional about priorities for in-person and phone patrons. Who is given highest priority? If the telephone rings while the paraprofessional is helping a patron at the reference desk, should the paraprofessional ignore the phone completely, leave the patron to answer it immediately, or leave the patron to answer the phone when the interview is finished? If the paraprofessional is looking for an answer for someone who called on the phone, and a patron with a question arrives, should they be asked to wait, or is the phone question dropped and answered later?

NONVERBAL CLUES

Desirable nonverbal cues to exhibit while providing reference service:

- Make eye contact
- Smile
- Good posture
- Friendly tone of voice
- Stand up
- Display genuine interest
- Appear confident
- Be patient
- Be courteous

LISTENING TESTS

QUESTION: An archaeologist claims he has dug up a coin that is clearly dated 46B.C. Why is he a liar?

ANSWER: B.C. means "Before Christ," and no one could have guessed when Christ would be born.

QUESTION: According to international law, if an airplane should crash on the exact border between two countries, would unidentified survivors be buried in the country they were traveling to, or the country they were traveling from?

ANSWER: No law allows you to bury survivors.

From John W. Newstrom. *Games Trainers Play*. New York: McGraw-Hill, 1980.

Finally, the paraprofessional should be encouraged to avoid conversations with other staff or patrons that are not related to reference questions. Patrons will believe that library staff are not available to assist them if they see staff members involved in personal conversations while on duty.

The nonverbal cues related to reference interviewing are also important. Suggest that the paraprofessional look up often so that he or she is aware of all patrons who are within sight of the reference desk. If the paraprofessional is given tasks to do while at the reference desk, he or she should be reminded to focus on patrons first rather than becoming very engrossed in the work. Avoid giving paraprofessionals tasks to complete at the reference desk that have firm deadlines that cannot be reasonably met. If the paraprofessional believes your task is more important or urgent than helping patrons, service will be impaired.

Paraprofessionals should make eye contact with every patron who approaches the reference desk. This indicates to the patron a willingness and interest in helping. A smile at this point is also important. Then the paraprofessional should offer assistance with the opening line generally used by your staff such as "Hello. May I help you?" or "May I help you find something?" By this time, the paraprofessional should have put down anything he or she was working with—pen, book, etc.—and should have changed positions so that he or she is completely facing the patron. This signals to the patron that he or she has the full attention of the paraprofessional.

As the question is asked, the paraprofessional moves into the listening phase of the reference interview. Stress to the paraprofessional that this is probably the most important part of the interview. If he or she misses some piece of information or clue about the question at this point, the wrong answer or no answer may be found. The paraprofessional should focus on what the patron is asking until the whole question is stated. Encourage the paraprofessional to think about his or her response after the question is asked instead of during the question. When the patron stops talking, the paraprofessional can say, "Let me think for a moment..." and then consider possible strategies and sources to use to answer the question.

If the paraprofessional tries to think about the answer and listen at the same time, a number of problems can occur. The paraprofessional might stop listening and thereby miss some important piece of information provided by the patron. If the patron senses the paraprofessional is not listening, he or she may stop talking

SAMPLE ROLE PLAY

Ask the paraprofessional to pretend to be a patron who wants to know how much ivory is produced from one set of elephant tusks, but only asks, "Where are your books about elephants?"

You pretend to be a reference staff member who cannot ask an open ended question. You might ask things such as:

- Do you need books or magazines?

- Do you want to know about their habitat or their reproduction?

- Do you want children's books or adult books?

- Do you want recent or older information?

- Do you want to know about them in zoos, in the wild or if they are endangered?

Several examples like this will help the paraprofessional see that closed questions are often not very helpful to the patron or the reference staff member. Try the question again using open ended questions such as:

- Can you tell me more about what you need?

- What exactly are you looking for?

- We have a number of books about elephants, can you be more specific?

- I don't believe I know what this is(means). Can you give me some more information?

- How will you use this information?

and end up withholding some useful piece of information. The patron might assume the paraprofessional is not interested or is unwilling to answer the question. If the paraprofessional does not hear the entire question correctly, he or she may answer the wrong question—the question he or she heard rather than the one that was asked. Or the paraprofessional, in his or her rush to answer the question, might actually interrupt the patron.

INTERVIEW STRATEGIES

Point out to the paraprofessional that during the reference interview, he or she may need to learn the answers to the following questions:

1. What does the user want to know?

Patrons are often unclear about their information needs for various reasons. They may feel uncomfortable about using the library or believe their question is "stupid." They may want to work independently, think the reference staff member will not understand what is needed, or expect the library does not have what is needed. Patrons often do not or cannot verbalize exactly what they need. And, sometimes, patrons do not even know exactly what they need. It is important that the paraprofessional take time to determine the patron's actual question.

There are several different methods to accomplish this. One of the most time efficient questions is to ask the patron, "What *exactly* do you want?" When patrons are clear about their information needs, this method will work well. Otherwise, the paraprofessional may need to ask more leading questions of the patron. These should be open-ended questions to encourage the patron to provide as much information as he or she has about the topic or question. Effective open-ended questions include:

- Can you tell me more about what you need?

- We have a number of books about _____. Perhaps you could be a bit more specific?

- I don't believe I know what _____ is/means. Can you give me some more information?

- How will you use this information?

The opposite of an open-ended question is a closed question, which gives the patron the option of answering yes, no, or selecting between several options. For example, questions such as:

- Is this needed for a class assignment or personal research?
- Do you need information about the legal or social aspects of marriage?
- Do you want a history of IBM? Or do you need figures on employees and financial status?

Closed questions make the reference interview a game of 20 questions in which the librarian tries to guess what the patron needs. Open-ended questions, on the other hand, allow the patron to tell the librarian everything he or she knows about the topic, and to explain the need as explicitly as possible.

As you discuss open-ended questions, give the paraprofessional examples of a number of standard responses so that he or she can choose or adapt one or two with which he or she feels most comfortable. It is necessary for the paraprofessional to find out exactly what the patron needs in order to provide the correct information.

2. In what form(s) (e.g. books, articles, videos) does the patron want the information?

Often patrons need more than one type of information. Explain to the paraprofessional the uses of different kinds of information. For example, books may be needed for historical information or to get background information on a topic. Periodical articles may be needed for current information or to go into detail about a topic. General or subject encyclopedias are helpful for providing background information about a topic. Ready reference sources will provide patrons with specific or factual information.

3. How much information does the patron want?

Explain that the amount of time that the paraprofessional spends with the patron will vary depending on the amount of information needed and the ease in finding that information. For example, if a patron needs information for a two or three page report, perhaps an encyclopedia article and a few periodical articles would suffice. A patron needing material for a 25-page paper will require quite a bit of information and probably much more help in finding it. In this case, the paraprofessional may want to point the patron to books, several periodical indexes, and a topical bibliography. If the need is for a specific piece of information, it may be found relatively quickly in one of a few ready reference sources such as *Information Please Almanac, Facts on File,* or the *Statistical Abstract of the United States.*

4. How much does he or she already know about the subject?

You should explain to the paraprofessional that the information sources used may vary considerably depending on the patron's prior knowledge of the subject. For example, patrons who need medical information may be at very different levels of understanding of medicine. A person who does not know much about the topic will need to use a medical guide that is geared to lay people. A nursing student or a medical professional will want to get his or her information from a nursing or medical source, perhaps a handbook, manual, or a scholarly medical journal.

It is vital for the paraprofessional to determine what prior knowledge the patron has about the topic as much for the sake of good public relations for the library as for the sake of finding correct information. For example, you do not want medical professionals to become insulted if the paraprofessional directs them to a drug source intended for lay people such as *The Pill Book.* On the other hand, you do not want a patron who is unfamiliar with medical terminology to become overwhelmed and frustrated if he or she is directed to *Physician's Desk Reference.*

5. Why does he or she want to know?

Although many library staff members find this question awkward to ask patrons, it is sometimes very helpful in determining their information needs and how to best meet those needs. For example, three patrons asking about a specific company may want the information for completely different reasons. One patron may be writing a research paper about the company and need background, historical, and current information about the company. Perhaps another patron owns stock in the company and simply needs the most recent stock information. A third patron may be preparing for an interview at the company and need current

GAINING INDEPENDENCE

When the paraprofessional begins answering reference questions on his or her own, avoid the temptation to step in and provide the answer. Let the paraprofessional work it through or come to you with questions. If the paraprofessional is hesitant to answer questions alone, try to take a consulting role. Ask open ended questions—

- "Where do *you* think the answer might be?"

- "Where have you already looked for an answer?"

- "Do you remember a question similar to this one that was asked last week? How did we answer that one?"

- You may not always be available to provide backup for the paraprofessional, so it is very important that the paraprofessional quickly becomes confident answering questions.

information about the company, including number of employees, ranking in the industry, and financial data. The reference search will be much more focused if the paraprofessional knows why the information is needed.

SPECIFIC COMMUNICATION PROBLEMS

1. The question is *garbled or unintelligible*.

Point out to the paraprofessional that there are several reasons that a question could be unintelligible. Perhaps the patron is foreign born and his or her English is difficult to understand. Maybe he or she has a speech impediment. Or it could be that the patron simply does not have strong verbal skills. In any case, you need to emphasize to the paraprofessional tolerance for and patience with patrons who may have special needs.

One strategy is to have the paraprofessional repeat back to the patron what he or she thinks the patron has said. The patron then can restate his or her request if the paraprofessional has misunderstood. Using this type of give-and-take conversation with the patron, it is often possible to come to understand an otherwise unintelligible information request. However, if the paraprofessional feels that he or she is simply not able to understand the patron, encourage the paraprofessional to refer the patron to another reference staff member.

2. The question is *vague, too broad, or overgeneralized*.

Often patrons do not know exactly what they need, are not sure how to verbalize their topic, or do not realize how much information is available about their topic. In this case, the paraprofessional is presented with a request such as, "I need information on World War II." The amount of information on World War II that many libraries have would be overwhelming for both the patron and the paraprofessional.

It is a good idea to check to determine if a more specific topic is desired by asking questions like, "What exactly do you need?" or "What is your area of interest related to the war?". Perhaps the patron wants to write a paper on the French resistance movement, a much more manageable topic. The paraprofessional needs to take the time to ask questions that will draw the real question out of the patron. Suggest that the paraprofessional ask the patron "If you found the perfect book or article about this subject, what do you think the title of it would be?" This is one way to lead the patron toward expressing his or her need and helping the paraprofessional to understand exactly what that need is. With the proper information, a successful reference search can follow.

There are also patrons who have not narrowed down their topic. Sometimes a student is given a broad topic to research for a term paper, but may not be familiar with how to narrow down a topic. Here, the paraprofessional should help the student by demonstrating research strategy methods. For example, the patron can get background information on the topic by using general encyclopedias. This can help to determine a specific area of the subject to research. Also, encyclopedias often have bibliographies that may be useful for the patron. They will then need to know that they can find background information by looking for books in the library's catalog, and current information by looking for articles in periodical or newspaper indexes. Other potential sources of information, such as pamphlets, government documents, or media can also be suggested.

3. The patron *assumes* the library staff has specialized knowledge.

Some patrons may phrase their reference questions using terms that are specific to a field or area of knowledge. Reference staff, who are often generalists or have in-depth knowledge in only one subject area, may not be able to decipher the information the patron needs. In this case, the paraprofessional needs to get more information from the patron. Perhaps the patron asks a paraprofessional for information regarding an overbreadth doctrine, and the paraprofessional has never heard the term. Questions that the paraprofessional needs to ask include:

- Can you give me some information about this?
- In what context was this used?
- If this is for a class, which class or what subject area?

The paraprofessional needs to at least determine the subject area of the question. If the patron does not know what the word or phrase means, the paraprofessional needs to get him or her to talk about it and tell the paraprofessional everything that is known about it. Sometimes the paraprofessional will need to look up the term in a dictionary or specialized encyclopedia before being able to find more information.

FACT VERSUS INFERENCE

Hold up an ordinary object, such as a book, pen, etc. Ask the paraprofessional to make statements of fact about the object. Record the statements. After getting about ten statements, point out any that go beyond that which can be observed. These are inferences rather than facts.

Ask how knowing something rather than inferring something might affect a reference interview. Discuss the importance of distinguishing between facts and inferences before responding to a request.

From John W. Newstrom. *More Games Trainers Play*. New York; McGraw-Hill, 1983.

THE GOLF BALL QUESTION

"It was the sixteenth hole in the Bob Hope Desert Classic, and the tall, handsome newcomer had an excellent chance of winning. His iron shot fell just short of the green, giving him a good chance for a birdie. Smiling broadly, he strode down the fairway only to stop in dismay. His ball had rolled into a small paper bag carelessly tossed on the ground by someone in the gallery.

If he removed the ball from the bag, it would cost him a penalty stroke. If he tried to hit the ball and the bag, he would lose control over the shot. What should he do? How can we solve this problem? What is one approach? (Get the ball out of the bag.) What is another way to state the problem? (Get the bag away from the ball.)"

Discuss with the paraprofessional the value of creative thinking when answering reference questions and the need, at times, to look at the question from a different perspective. There may be no penalty-free way for the golfer to get the ball out of the bag but from another perspective, it may be possible to remove the bag from the ball. Especially if a match is available to burn the bag!

From John W. Newstrom. *Games Trainers Play*. New York; McGraw-Hill, 1980.

4. The patron has *incomplete* or *incorrect information.*

This problem can take several forms. Perhaps a patron does not know the exact title of a book he or she wants, or the information that the patron does have is not completely correct. Here again, it is important to establish a dialogue. For example, a patron may ask for a book called *Ten New Directions of Transforming Life* when he or she really wants the book *Megatrends: Ten New Directions Transforming Our Lives*. The paraprofessional might start by asking, "What else do you know about this book?" If the patron does not respond to this, have the paraprofessional ask the patron more specific questions, such as "Do you know who wrote the book?", "Do you know what this book is about?", or "Is this for a class assignment? What class?" Suggest that the paraprofessional try to get the patron to talk about the book and get clues from any additional information that is provided.

Another patron may ask for a definition of corpus habeas instead of habeas corpus. Again, have the paraprofessional find out as much as he or she can about the question. Paraprofessionals need to know that patrons do sometimes provide incorrect information.

5. The patron asks for a *specific source*, and does not indicate exactly what information is needed.

In some cases, patrons may have information about the sources that they need to use. However, unless they already know how to use the source, it is not enough to simply direct them to the shelf. For example, a patron may ask, "Where is *Psychological Abstracts*?" The paraprofessional needs to ask the patron if he or she knows how to use the source and what kind of information he or she needs. Then, depending on the library, the paraprofessional may get the information for the patron or instruct him or her in the use of the source. In this way, the patron is not left to muddle around in *Psychological Abstracts*, possibly becoming frustrated and leaving the library without an answer to his or her question.

Another possibility is that the patron mentions one source when perhaps another source would be more appropriate for his or her topic. For example, a patron may ask where the *Physician's Desk Reference* is, and actually want information about an over-the-counter drug. If the paraprofessional asks the patron to describe the information he or she needs, the paraprofessional will know that that book would not be the best source to answer the question. Rather, the *Physician's Desk Reference for Nonprescription Drugs* would be more appropriate for the patron's question.

SEARCH STRATEGIES

Part of conducting a successful reference interview is analyzing the question in light of the library's resources. One way to demonstrate this to paraprofessionals is to introduce them to the concept of reference search strategies. Indicate that an important aspect of reference work is pursuing search strategies that are consistent with the questions asked. To become more adept at the search strategy, paraprofessionals may want to use the worksheet shown in Figure 5-2.

1. Can the answer be determined by consulting a library bibliography, subject guide, or pathfinder? Introduce the paraprofessional to any pathfinders prepared by your staff. Point out where they are stored and who decides when one is needed. These resources can be extremely valuable because they have been developed with your library and community in mind. Often they will list the most useful sources for some of your most common questions and will help the paraprofessional remember the best sources in which to begin a search.

2. Can the answer be determined with a ready reference work? These works are useful to check for factual information; common examples would be *Information Please Almanac* and *Famous First Facts*. You will want to make sure the paraprofessional is comfortable using all of the materials in your ready reference collection.

3. Can the answer be determined from an encyclopedia article? Remind paraprofessionals of the usefulness of encyclopedia articles for background information. They also often contain useful bibliographies, which may lead to more information available in your collection. The introduction provided by an encyclopedia may help a patron narrow his or her search, or otherwise refine his or her request.

Figure 5-2

REFERENCE INTERVIEW WORKSHEET

As you observe and begin to answer reference questions, consider these steps:

Question:

Do any words need to be defined?

What discipline, field, subject area?

How much information is needed?

What time period?

How recent does the information need to be?

What format is needed?

What level of information is needed?

Sources to consult:

Library pathfinders/bibliographies/subject guides

Ready reference sources

Encyclopedias

Other reference sources

Library catalog

Indexes

Subject bibliography

Refer questions with which you have difficulty to another staff member.

4. Can the answer be determined by consulting a reference source? You will want to make sure the paraprofessional is familiar with materials in your reference collection. Training in reference sources is discussed in more detail in Chapter 6. It is also important that the paraprofessional be familiar with the classification scheme used in your library so that he or she can browse the shelves in search of an answer if he or she is unfamiliar with a specific title that might answer the question.

5. Can the answer be determined by consulting the library's catalog? If a patron needs a specific book, the paraprofessional should check the catalog first by author or title to determine if the library owns the book, and if so, its location. If the item is a reference book, the paraprofessional may want to accompany the patron to the reference stacks to help the patron use the book. If the book is not in the catalog at all, the paraprofessional will want to ask if the patron would like to get the book through interlibrary loan. If a patron is looking for information about a specific topic, the paraprofessional can check the catalog under the correct subject heading. If the catalog is able to provide keyword searching, it can be a "quick and dirty" way to determine appropriate subject headings for the topic. Catalog training is discussed further in Chapter 6.

6. Can the answer be determined by consulting indexes? Encourage the paraprofessional to make use of the indexes, and emphasize that he or she should not be afraid to learn while doing. A brief look at the introductory material may help determine how to best use an index. And, showing the patron how to use an index will make future research easier for him or her.

7. Can the answer be determined with a subject bibliography (a published book providing a list of sources on a specific topic)? A subject bibliography is useful for pointing patrons to further information on a topic. Often subject bibliographies list both periodical articles and books on a topic. Help the paraprofessional understand the connection between bibliographies and your collection either by using the library catalog or the library periodical holdings list.

Often, an answer to a reference question will lend itself to a variety of sources that are available at the library—books, periodical articles, reference sources, etc. Encourage the paraprofessional to try several different types of sources to answer a reference question.

As the paraprofessional searches for an answer, he or she should keep the patron informed of what is being done by saying something such as "I think the encyclopedia article about ____ should give us this information. Follow me while we check." If a number of steps will be involved, encourage the paraprofessional to briefly summarize them for the patron what needs to be before beginning the search. For example: "To locate current articles about ____, we will need to check the ____ index. That will give us references to magazine articles so then we will check the library periodical holdings list. From there you will go to the magazines area on the ____ floor. The indexes are over here. Please follow me." This helps the patron realize the answer will not be available in the first source he or she consults. The paraprofessional should also avoid using jargon or acronyms when helping patrons. Phrases such as "docs," "stacks," or *LCSH* may be unfamiliar and unhelpful terms for most patrons.

You will want to encourage the paraprofessional to rely on other reference staff for referrals. Remind the paraprofessional that serving the patron is the first priority. Who finds the answer or where it is found is of less importance than making sure an answer is found. Recommend that when the paraprofessional refers a question, he or she either follow along as the question is answered, or, after the staff member completes his or her interaction with the patron, ask how the question was answered.

CLOSING THE REFERENCE INTERVIEW

After interaction with the patron has taken place, make sure that the paraprofessional knows how to close the reference interview. It is important that patrons know that they can return to a library staff member for further assistance either if more information is needed or if they were not able to locate exactly what they wanted. Paraprofessionals should ask the patron, "Does this completely answer your question? Is this what you want?" Paraprofessionals should also inform the patron to check back with them or another reference staff member if more information is needed. Part of a good reference interview is making patrons feel comfortable with asking reference questions in the future.

It is important for paraprofessionals to be trained in reference interviewing techniques. Without knowing how to communicate with patrons, paraprofessionals will not be able to answer reference questions. When they are accomplished at the reference interview, paraprofessionals will not only be more successful in answering reference questions, they will also provide good public relations for the library. Satisfied patrons will feel comfortable in using the library again and asking for help if they need it.

RESOURCES

Edmonds, Leslie, and Ellen D. Sutton. "The Reference Interview" in *Reference and Information Services: An Introduction.* ed. by Richard E. Bopp and Linda C. Smith, 42-58. Englewood Cliffs, CO: Libraries Unlimited, 1991. Edmonds and Sutton discuss the reference interview, covering verbal and nonverbal communication, questioning, locating the answer, and describe several types of reference interviews.

Gothberg, Helen M. "Managing Difficult People: Patrons (and Others)." *The Reference Librarian* 19 (1987): 269-283. Gothberg describes types of difficult patrons and discusses how to deal with hostile aggressives, silent unresponsives, indecisives, and know-it-all experts.

Goulding, Mary. "Real Librarians Don't Play 'Jeopardy'." *Illinois Libraries* 73 (February 1991): 140-146. Goulding argues that "pride of place" inhibits reference service and that reference staff should focus on what is needed to answer the question rather than on sources available in the library.

Nolan, Christopher W. "Closing the Reference Interview: Implications for Policy and Practice." *RQ* 31 (Summer 1992): 513-523. Nolan identifies the importance of closing the reference interview and examines the goals of the patron and library employee in the interview. He suggests policies and training ideas to ensure successful reference interviews.

Schwartz, Diane G., and Dottie Eakin. "Reference Service Standards, Performance Criteria, and Evaluation." *The Journal of Academic Librarianship*. 12 (March 1986): 4-8. Alfred Taubman Medical Library, at the University of Michigan, identified qualities of good reference service in their attempt to begin evaluating reference librarian performance. They created a "Checklist of Reference Skills" to evaluate reference staff and developed a "Reference Work Sheet" to record time-consuming reference questions for use in future training and staff development.

Yates, Rochelle. *A Librarian's Guide to Telephone Reference Service*. Hamden, CT: Library Professional Publications, 1986. Yates provides information about giving reference service over the phone, including the reference interview, ready reference collection, and training. She includes approximately 80 practice reference questions.

6 TRAINING MODULES

After the paraprofessional is familiar with conducting reference interviews, the supervisor must begin training the paraprofessional to use reference sources. Providing training takes a great deal of time and planning, but the process can be broken down into steps. You need to:

1. Identify what training is needed;
2. Organize the training into logical segments;
3. Prepare the training modules;
4. Present the training;
5. Evaluate its effect; and
6. Revise the training for future use.

This chapter will cover the organization and objectives of training, the use of pretests, and training module design.

ORGANIZATION

Initially, the supervisor must create an overview of all of the training that the paraprofessional will need in order to perform well at the reference desk. Much of this work should have been done during the planning stages before the paraprofessional was hired. You can make a list of all of the resources the paraprofessional should know how to use when his or her training is complete. These can be grouped by type (encyclopedias, atlases, local experts, area libraries, etc.) or by subject (current events, business, careers, etc.). Next these should be ranked by importance (see the discussion of sequencing in Chapter 2). The paraprofessional probably needs to understand how to use the library's catalog before being introduced to *Readers' Guide to Periodical Literature* or any Standard and Poor's Corporation publications. You can also consider the time of year when training will be provided, because this may affect when information will need to be presented. For example, if the paraprofessional begins work in May, an introduction to the library's travel information section might be more timely than an introduction to the library's resources on Native Americans, which are most heavily used at Thanksgiving time. All of the training does not have to be presented within the first three to four months on the job. If the supervisor knows that questions about Indians are asked every November, training in Indian sources can be provided in November even if the paraprofessional begins work in May and completes all other training in August.

You should also consider including training in resources beyond the library. If libraries in nearby cities or local experts are contacted for some questions, the paraprofessional should be made aware of these resources and any procedures that are to be followed when contacting these sources.

OBJECTIVES

Before you begin preparing a training module related to a specific subject or type of reference source, you will need written instructional objectives for the session. As discussed in Chapter 2, instructional objectives indicate what the paraprofessional should know when training is complete. Instructional objectives also provide information about what conditions may affect the activity to be learned and how well the activity is to be performed.

You should have written objectives for the areas in which training is needed during the planning process. Refer to these to determine the best way to prepare the paraprofessional to provide service. You may also have identified other areas in which training is needed since the original planning, and instructional objectives can be written for these topics as well.

PRETEST

After identifying areas in which the paraprofessional needs training and writing instructional objectives related to each area, you can move on to determining what the paraprofessional already knows. The experience of new paraprofessionals must be taken into consideration when developing training sessions. A new employee who has worked in libraries before may not need to spend much time learning how to use the catalog or when to use basic reference sources. Administering a pretest can help you determine what level and amount of training will best prepare the paraprofessional for the job. A pretest includes questions about resources that the paraprofessional will need to know how to use. The paraprofessional's performance on the pretest will indicate what areas you need to cover and in how much detail. The pretest can also be used again after training is complete to see how much the paraprofessional has learned. This will be discussed further in Chapter 8.

When creating the pretest, you must first define its purpose. Presumably it will be used to identify areas in which the paraprofessional needs training. The pretest also alerts the paraprofessional to what will be important on the job. The supervisor must decide how much information the pretest will cover. You can either use one wide-ranging pretest covering everything the paraprofessional will know at the end of the training, or a pretest can be given before each section of training (e.g., library catalog, general reference sources, indexes, subject-specific reference sources, etc.).

Using the list of important resources you have developed, you can design questions that will determine how much knowledge the paraprofessional already has about selected sources. Combinations of fill-in-the-blanks, multiple choice, and matching questions can be used. After the questions have been developed, write directions to be included in the pretest. Be sure to explain that it is diagnostic and that the paraprofessional should avoid guessing at answers. Another staff member should review the test to look for questions that may be too difficult or irrelevant. For example, knowing the history of the Dewey Decimal System is probably irrelevant in most libraries, but understanding that call numbers relate to the subject of a book is vital. (A sample pretest is given in the following subject catalog module.)

After the paraprofessional has completed the test and you have graded it, you should briefly review all of the questions and answers with him or her. This will reinforce the knowledge the paraprofessional already has. You can also promise training in areas where the test indicates the paraprofessional needs it. Incorrect knowledge needs to be corrected immediately. Both the library and the paraprofessional will want to avoid a situation where a paraprofessional unknowingly provides incorrect information. For example, the paraprofessional might be confused about "see" and "see also" references. If the paraprofessional indicates he or she knows nothing about these references, the supervisor could expect the paraprofessional to refer any questions about them to professional librarians. However, if the paraprofessional mistakenly believes he or she understands the use of "see" and "see also" references, he or she will probably not refer patrons to a professional.

DESIGNING TRAINING MODULES

The goal in training is to enable the paraprofessional to handle patron questions, whether by providing an answer or a referral when professional librarians cannot be at the reference desk. One effective way to do this is to select a group of resources with which the paraprofessional must be familiar and provide practice questions that can be answered using these important sources. The process covered in this chapter involves organizing training into separate modules.

A training module consists of a handout discussing a type or group of sources with a set of practice questions and answers. Training modules can be prepared for specific sources, tasks, and subject areas. Organizing training into modules is helpful because it forces the supervisor to provide information in manageable and logical sections. Without the imposed limitations of training modules, you may be inclined to simply walk to the shelves, point to a book and say, "We use this one for x; this one for y." This type of orientation does not allow the paraprofessional to examine important sources or practice using them. The training module also gives the paraprofessional something to which he or she can refer when patrons ask questions.

Training modules about common reference sources, such as indexes, encyclopedias, or atlases, may contain a great deal of narrative explaining how and why a particular source is used. Training modules for subject areas typically include a handout prepared by the supervisor that includes a descriptive list of sources, a set of practice questions, and their answers. Training modules can also include sample pages from the sources themselves or copies of handouts that are given to patrons.

You can work from memory and experience in identifying commonly asked questions or often used sources. You can also ask other reference staff members to record reference questions and appropriate resources over the course of several weeks. These questions and sources can be examined to select topics, sources,

HELPFUL SOURCES

Other sources you can consult for descriptions of reference sources and sample reference questions or worksheets include:

Bopp, Richard E., and Linda C. Smith. *Reference and Information Services: An Introduction.* Englewood, CO: Libraries Unlimited, 1991.

Gates, Jean Key. *Guide to the Use of Libraries and Information Sources.* 6th ed. New York: McGraw-Hill, 1989.

Hauer, Mary G. et al. *Books, Libraries, and Research.* 3d ed. Dubuque, IA: Kendall-Hunt, 1990.

Slavens, Thomas P. *Information Interviews and Questions.* Metuchen, NJ: The Scarecrow Press, Inc., 1978.

Taylor, Margaret T., and Ronald R. Powell. *Basic Reference Sources: A Self-Study Manual.* 4th ed. Metuchen, NJ: The Scarecrow Press, 1990.

and practice questions. Training modules should include any sources that reference staff normally use including reference books, main collection materials, and resource people or libraries. The training modules should emphasize the resources most commonly used by reference staff.

When possible, common subject areas should be identified (e.g. business, current events, resumes/job seeking, animals, science, government, etc.). Training modules should be prepared for the major subject categories identified by reference staff. After identifying the most important sources, you can examine each one and prepare a brief description about the information in it that is most needed by your library patrons. Anything important or out of the ordinary about arrangement, scope, indexing, etc. should also be noted. Select a typical question for which the source would be used and find the answer in the source and note its page number. Write all of this down for use in the handouts.

When you've gathered enough material, prepare a handout that provides the bibliographic information about each source, its location and call number, and a brief description. Also create a separate list of practice questions and answers. It may be helpful to separate the questions and answers, or even to seal the answers in an envelope to be opened only after the paraprofessional has tried to answer the questions.

Give the paraprofessional the handout and questions. Show the paraprofessional the source on the shelf and provide an overview of its scope, purpose, and arrangement and offer examples of when the source can be used. When all of the sources in a given training module have been reviewed, give the paraprofessional an opportunity to answer the practice questions and check his or her responses against your prepared answers. You should be available to answer questions and review any sources as necessary.

The following pages provide examples of training modules. The first deals with the use of the subject catalog. The objectives, pretest, handout, and practice questions are provided. Because the answers for these questions will vary in each library, no answers are provided for this module. Following the subject catalog session are modules about general encyclopedias, book reviews, InfoTrac, *PsycLit,* business information, current events, and information about the government. The last six sessions contain objectives, handouts, practice questions, and answers. These are intended as samples to help you prepare handouts to be used by paraprofessionals in your library.

TRAINING TIPS

- Consider having the paraprofessional meet with someone from your cataloging staff for a more in-depth introduction to cataloging practices such as main entries, authority work, and call number creation.

- Or have the paraprofessional "catalog" a book. Give him or her a book and a sample main entry record for a different book. Ask the paraprofessional to create a main entry for the book. This allows him or her to see where all of the information in the catalog record comes from.

MODULE 1: Catalog Training

PREPARATION

Catalogs in libraries differ greatly today because of online public access catalogs. It is therefore difficult to provide a complete discussion about preparing paraprofessionals to use catalogs. The checklist below is intended to help you consider some of the topics that might be covered in a discussion about using a catalog whether the format is cards, microfilm, microfiche, or online.

It is useful to give the paraprofessional sample records from the catalog and point out differences in the information on a record based on where the record comes from—for example, main entry, subject entry, or item in circulation. Following this checklist is a sample pretest to use to see what paraprofessionals know about using a subject catalog. A handout relating to the subject catalog and a number of sample practice questions are also provided.

CHECKLIST

1. What is the purpose of the catalog?

   Index to the book collection of this library

2. What is represented in the catalog?

   Books

   Periodicals

   Audiovisual materials

   Government documents

   Pamphlet file materials

   Holdings of other libraries

   Books purchased/cataloged since a particular date

   Books cataloged with Library of Congress or Dewey Decimal call numbers

3. How is the information in the catalog accessed?

   Author

   Title

   Subject

   Keyword

   Call number

   Other access points

SUBJECT CATALOG TRAINING HANDOUT

Libraries depend on their catalogs to help patrons determine what books they own. There are at least two entries in the catalog for every book the library owns—one under author and one under title. For a nonfiction book, there will also be subject entries, which help locate answers to questions such as "Do you have any books about trees?" To answer this question, the patron should look in the subject section of the catalog under "trees."

Once the patron finds the section of the catalog that discusses trees, he or she will have to interpret the entry. The number in the upper left-hand corner of the record is the book's call number. This number is used to locate the books on the shelf. The record also gives the author's name, title, publisher, place of publication, and copyright date for the book. The card indicates how many pages are in the book and if it includes any illustrations, bibliographies, or indexes. The record also lists subject headings that have been assigned to the book. There are often three or four subject headings. These subject headings can be useful if the patron cannot find what he or she needs in the "trees" section. He or she can try using one of the other subject headings assigned to some "tree" books.

Sometimes the patron will find a record that says to "see" another subject. This means the subject the patron started with is not used in the catalog, but that books can be located under the suggested heading. It would be impossible for the library to have records for every subject every patron might want to use. For example, there are a great many synonyms for "car," including automobile, vehicle, motor vehicle, and auto. For simplicity, the library selects one of these terms, "automobiles," and puts all books about cars under this subject heading. "See" records are added to the catalog for synonyms of "automobiles." All of the proper subject headings and many of their improper synonyms are listed in the subject headings books.

The library also uses "see also" records. These records are used when the library owns books on the chosen topic and topics related to it. For example, if the patron looked under "trees," he or she might be directed to "see also", "shrubs", and "plants." Books about shrubs or plants might provide additional useful information about trees for the patron.

4. Where can the catalog be used?
    Main library
    Branch libraries
    Any terminal in building
    Other libraries in a consortium
    Dial access
    Internet
    Special hours of online access
5. Special features
    Keyword searching
    Boolean operators
    Browse items nearby on shelf
    Redo search in different database without rekeying
    Periodical indexes with same search commands
    Placing holds/recalls
    Leaving messages for library
6. Searching for authors
    Last name first
    Alphabetical order
    Mc and Mac arrangement
    Authority file
    Pseudonyms
    Misspellings
    Display order (alphabetical or chronological)
7. Searching for titles
    Omit "a," "an," "the" if first word of a title
    Misspellings
    Display order (alphabetical or chronological)
8. Searching for subjects
    Subject authority
    Subject headings list
    Subject subdivisions

TRAINING TIPS

- Explain the importance of subject access to the collection.
- Point out that title and author searches are generally straight forward but subject searching can get quite complex.
- The paraprofessional should be comfortable using the catalog when you begin to discuss subject headings and the subject heading list. Provide a few of your favorite "subject headings no one ever thinks of" as examples.
- Encourage the paraprofessional to be creative when using the subject catalog.
- Develop practice questions that reflect the common, tricky searches in your library and have the paraprofessional practice with them.

Alphabetical order

Misspellings

Display order (alphabetical or chronological)

Cross references

9. Searching for keywords

What is a keyword

MARC record tags used in keyword search

Turning keyword search into subject search

10. How to read a record

Call numbers

Locations

Circulation

Bibliographic information

Status messages (missing, lost, at bindery)

Periodical records (current issues available)

SUBJECT CATALOG TRAINING OBJECTIVES

1. From memory, correctly identify all parts of the subject catalog entry.

2. Using any available resources, correctly answer 90 percent of all questions about subject headings.

3. Using any available resources, correctly answer 90 percent of questions involving "see" and "see also" references.

4. Using the catalog and the subject headings list, correctly find books by subject 90 percent of the time.

SUBJECT CATALOG PRETEST

DIRECTIONS: This test is designed to indicate how much you already know about the subject catalog, and in what areas you will need training. For this reason, do not guess at answers; if you do not know the answer, simply leave that question blank. Some questions may require more than one answer.

1. Every book has at least _____ entries in the catalog.

2. Books are grouped in the catalog by ____:
   a. date purchased   b. title
   c. copyright date   d. subject/title
   e. author   f. author/title
   g. subject   h. publisher

3. Nonfiction books are shelved according to ____:
   a. date purchased   b. title
   c. color   d. call number
   e. author   f. height
   g. subject   h. publication date

4. Fiction books are shelved according to ____:
   a. call number   b. title
   c. author   d. subject
   e. publisher   f. height
   g. color   h. publication date

5. The book's call number is found in the lower right hand corner of the catalog entry.
   True____ or False____

6. Every nonfiction book is assigned a(n) ____:
   a. call number   b. purchase order number
   c. phone number   d. address

7. The call number represents the book's ____:
   a. author   b. title
   c. subject   d. publication date
   e. price   f. size
   g. location   h. color

8. Each nonfiction book will be listed in the catalog by ____:
   a. date of purchase   b. subject
   c. call number   d. title
   e. author   f. chapter title
   g. publication date   h. publisher

9. There is a list of approved subject headings used in libraries.
   True____ or False____

10. A "see" reference tells you there are other books about your subject in the librarian's office.

   True_____ or False_____

11. A "see also" reference tells you that you looked under the wrong subject heading.

   True_____ or False_____

12. A nonfiction book is a made-up story.

   True_____ or False_____

13. How can you find out if this library owns a book about trees (without asking a librarian)?

   _____

   _____

14. Which of the following pieces of information can you find about a book by using the catalog?
   a. author   b. title
   c. publication date d. publisher
   e. height   f. number of pages
   g. illustrations   h. bibliographies
   i. indexes   j. subject
   k. location   l. all of the above

15. What items are not recorded in the catalog?
   a. magazines   b. films
   c. videos   d. microfilms
   e. dissertations   f. new books

16. The library uses subject headings chosen by_____:
   a. Melvil Dewey   b. Library of Congress
   c. Library Director d. Dr. Seuss
   e. Sears   f. Charles Cutter

PRACTICE QUESTIONS

   1. How many books do we own about trees?

   2. How will you find books about biplanes?

   3. What is the call number for a book about Shakespeare written by Smith?

   4. Where should you look for books about Russia?

5. Who is the author of the first book in the catalog about boats?

6. In what years were our books about horsebreaking published?

7. What subject headings are assigned to *The Train Book*?

8. How many of our books about rockets have bibliographies?

9. Do we have any oversize books about eleventh century Oriental art?

10. Under what subject headings do we have books about expert systems?

11. What is the subject heading for recent travel books about Paris?

TRAINING TIPS

- For this session, it may be most useful to have the paraprofessional do the encyclopedia comparison before you meet with him or her. The comparison very quickly points out differences between the sources and familiarizes paraprofessionals with the amount of information that encyclopedias provide.

- Meet with the paraprofessional immediately after the comparison and discuss his or her findings. Point out other differences and uses related to encyclopedias in your library. Then give the paraprofessional the handout and the practice questions to complete.

MODULE 2: Encyclopedia Training

OBJECTIVES

1. Using the volumes of different encyclopedias, identify differences in coverage of selected topics.

2. Using any encyclopedia, use the index volumes every time the encyclopedia is used.

ENCYCLOPEDIA COMPARISON

Your first handout related to encyclopedias asks you to compare our three encyclopedias so that you can begin to become familiar with the differences between them. After completing the comparison exercise below, you will be ready to try to answer the practice questions using the encyclopedias.

Compare entries in our three encyclopedias (*World Book Encyclopedia*, *Encyclopaedia Britannica*, *Encyclopedia Americana*) for the following categories. Write down the topic you are using for each category.

1. A country
2. A living person
3. A dead person
4. An animal
5. An occupation
6. A recent change (rulers of countries, boundary changes, country name changes, discoveries related to diseases or drugs, etc.)
7. A controversial topic
8. A US state

For each category, compare the information that is provided. Especially notice some of the following things:

- Does the index refer to other articles of interest?
- How is the encyclopedia alphabetized (letter-by-letter or word-by-word)?

- How many columns or pages are devoted to the topic?
- How much detail is given in the entry?
- Is the information up to date?
- Are there pictures, maps, or special features? Do they add to the information in the text?
- Are bibliographies provided?
- Are cross references to other articles given?
- For each category, is basic information easily located?

Following are some basic things that you can look for in each encyclopedia:

Country:
- Population
- Area
- Flag
- Motto
- President/governor
- Date established

Person:
- Birth/death date
- Importance of person
- Family history
- Relationship to other people important at the same time

Animal:
- Habitat
- Location
- Relationship to other animals
- Length of life
- Reproduction
- Eating habits

ENCYCLOPEDIA TRAINING HANDOUT

Encyclopedias provide a great deal of information about many topics. There is probably an entry in an encyclopedia for just about any topic in which someone might be interested. The encyclopedia is intended to give you a brief introduction to a topic. It will provide definitions, explanations, history, current status, statistics, and sometimes, a bibliography.

Encyclopedias are arranged in alphabetical order but you should always check the index for your topic. If there are several encyclopedia entries that deal with your topic, the index will identify those other important entries for you.

Often an encyclopedia is a good starting place if you or the patron do not know much about the topic. Because the encyclopedia identifies important people, dates, ideas, and definitions it can lead you to other reference sources, periodical indexes, or the catalog after you have learned a little bit about the subject.

The library owns several encyclopedias because each one has different strengths. Some provide a lot of information about selected topics while others cover many more topics in less depth. Some encyclopedias are written for students while others are intended for adults. Some provide good maps, information about recent events, controversial topics, or career information, and others omit some or all of this information.

Encyclopedias are reissued every year but they do not have to change every article every year to be given a new copyright date. Be aware that very recent information (within the last one to two years) will often not be correct in an encyclopedia. The easiest way to determine how much is changed from one year to the next is to compare page numbers between editions. If most entries seem to be on the same page when you compare the new edition with an old one, then you know the edition has not been changed significantly.

The Encylopedia Americana (Danbury, CT: Grolier, Inc. ISBN: 0-7172-0119-8) is a good encylopedia for United States information, especially history, geography, and biography. It provides short, factual articles rather than long discussions like *Encyclopaedia Britannica*.

The New Encyclopaedia Britannica (Chicago: Encyclopaedia Britannica. ISBN: 0-85229-529-4) provides extensive articles on many subjects in volumes called Macropaedia, and shorter entries in the volumes called Micropaedia. It is very important to use the index volumes to know for sure that you have located everything about your topic in *Britannica*.

The World Book Encyclopedia (Chicago: World Book. ISBN: 0-7166-1289-5) is a popular encyclopedia targeted to students. Its entries begin simply and progress to more complex ideas, and it uses vocabularies that make it useful for many people. It provides good coverage of social studies, science, biography, and occupations. In general, its illustrations and maps are quite good.

Occupation:
- Education needed
- Typical day
- Earnings
- Professional associations

Recent change:
- Correct information
- If not correct, is there any indication it might change (Upcoming elections? War taking place?)

Controversial topic:
- Is it included?
- Are two sides of the issue treated?
- Is the controversy mentioned?
- Is the opinion of the writer evident?

PRACTICE QUESTIONS

These questions should give you some experience using the encyclopedias. Try looking up each answer in at least two of our encyclopedias. Compare the answers that you find. Record the actual answer to each question as well as notes about the different information provided by each encyclopedia.

1. What two bodies of water are linked by the New York State Barge Canal?
2. What are the names of the provinces in the Netherlands?
3. Can you find a list of dates important to the westward movement in the United States?
4. Who were the Industrial Workers of the World?
5. Where and when did checkers begin?
6. Can you find a picture of a springbok?
7. What is the name of Michael Jackson's best selling album?
8. I'm interested in becoming a lawyer. Do you have any information about what lawyers do or what training they need?

9. What was Babe Ruth's real name?

10. What is the state flower of Mississippi?

11. When was the Battle of Chippewa fought?

12. When did Eli Whitney invent the cotton gin?

13. Where is James Polk buried?

ANSWERS TO PRACTICE QUESTIONS

1. *Encyclopaedia Britannica* identifies the Hudson River and Lake Erie as the two bodies of water linked by the New York State Barge Canal. *Encyclopedia Americana* provides a map that shows that several bodies of water are connected by the Barge Canal. *World Book Encyclopedia* provides no index entry for the Barge Canal.

2. Both *World Book Encyclopedia* and *Encyclopedia Americana* provide a list of provinces in the Netherlands in the index to their map of the country. *Encyclopaedia Britannica* provides an actual list in the supplemental volume called "World Data." The provinces are Drenthe, Flevoland, Friesland, Gelderland, Groningen, Limburg, Noord-Brabant, Noord-Holland, Overijssel, Utrecht, Zeeland, and Zuid-Holland.

3. *World Book Encyclopedia* provides a list of dates important to the U.S. westward movement to accompany nine pages of text under "westward movement." The other two encyclopedias provide text describing the westward movement but no explicit list of dates.

4. All three encyclopedias identify the Industrial Workers of the World as a radical labor organization founded in the early 1900s to oppose the American Federation of Labor.

5. Both *Encyclopaedia Britannica* and *Encyclopedia Americana* indicate checkers can be traced to 1600 BC. *World Book Encyclopedia* does not provide any information on this aspect of checkers.

6. *Encyclopaedia Britannica* and *World Book Encyclopedia* both provide color pictures of a springbok. *Encyclopedia Americana* has a black-and-white photo, and if you closely follow all the leads given in the *Americana* index you will find a second black-and-white picture in the South Africa article.

7. *World Book Encyclopedia* is the only encyclopedia of the three that includes Michael Jackson and it identifies his best selling album as *Thriller*.

8. *World Book Encyclopedia* is the most comprehensive source here—providing almost a whole page of information about the work and training of lawyers. *Encyclopedia Americana* gives lawyers one paragraph in a section about career planning. *Encyclopaedia Britannica* describes what lawyers do in a number of countries with the United States receiving one sentence.

9. *Encyclopaedia Britannica* makes this one easy by putting George Herman Ruth in the index under "Ruth, Babe." *World Book Encyclopedia* implies, in the entry about Ruth, that his full name is George Herman Ruth, while *Encyclopedia Americana* never identifies the real name.

10. All three encyclopedias identify the state flower of Mississippi as the magnolia. *World Book Encyclopedia* provides a color picture of the flower along with information about the state flag, seal, bird, and tree. *Encyclopaedia Britannica* provides the information in a chart with the state nickname, motto, tree, bird, and flower for all 50 states. *Encyclopedia Americana* provides a chart with the entry for each state giving information about location, elevation, area, population, climate, etc.

11. The Battle of Chippewa was fought on July 5, 1814, according to *Encyclopedia Americana* and *Encyclopaedia Britannica,* while *World Book Encyclopedia* implies that the Battle took place sometime in July 1814.

12. All three encyclopedias record 1793 as the date for Whitney's invention of the cotton gin. This information can be located by using either "Whitney" or "cotton gin" as an index entry.

13. According to *World Book Encyclopedia* and *Encyclopedia Americana,* Polk is buried in Nashville, Tennessee. *Encyclopaedia Britannica* does not include this piece of information.

TRAINING TIPS

- Several days before the *InfoTrac* training, encourage the paraprofessional to pay special attention to reference interviews that involve using *InfoTrac*.

- For the training session, start at the computer and explain to the paraprofessional how to use your equipment—booting; rebooting; menu choices; network protocols; etc.

- Have several searches ready for the paraprofessional to try as examples.

- Make sure the paraprofessional understands how to read the citations on the screen and understands the connection between the citations and your collection—periodical lists or the library catalog.

- Have the paraprofessional do the practice questions and read the handout as a review. If your library has prepared handouts for patrons, use these instead of preparing a new handout. In this way, the paraprofessional learns what information the patrons are seeing.

MODULE 3: InfoTrac: General Periodical Index Training

OBJECTIVES

1. Given a topic, locate at least one article by using *General Periodical Index* under subject heading or Expanded Search.

2. Correctly use the Expanded Search.

3. Using any available resources, correctly answer 75 percent of requests for current information using *General Periodical Index*.

PRACTICE QUESTIONS

1. Where can I find reviews of the movie "Basic Instinct"?

2. I heard something about a carjacking bill. Can you help me find any information about it?

3. I'm writing a paper about computer crimes and I'd like to describe some of them in it.

4. I'd like some information on the economic plans Ross Perot introduced during the 1992 presidential campaign.

5. How can I find which stereo would be best to buy?

6. I'm doing a paper on the famine in Somalia and I need recent magazine articles.

7. Are there any articles about models and their eating habits?

8. Where can I find articles about Michael Jackson and his life?

9. Where can I find reviews of *The Kitchen God's Wife*?

10. I'd like some information on the treatment of children who have AIDS.

INFOTRAC TRAINING HANDOUT

General Periodical Index is a CD-ROM which idexes articles from approximately 1,100 popular magazines and journals. It includes entries covering current events, consumer information, arts and entertainment, and business, management, and finance. Many citations include abstracts.

You can search *General Periodical Index* using the subject guide or the Expanded Search guide. The subject guide will match the topic chosen to the subject listing. Instructional windows will help you determine how to continue searching. Online instructions are always present at the bottom of the screen. Also, the template on the keyboard describes the most important function keys.

The Expanded Search allows you to combine two or more words or concepts in one search. The search functions, like keyword searching, looks for the chosen word(s) in the article title, subject headings, subheadings, and abstracts.

FUNCTION KEYS

General Peridodical Index's functions are controlled by the following keys:

F1—START/FINISH key: Allows you to begin a new search, select a different database, or terminate your search session.

F2—HELP: Displays additional instructions on how to use your CD-ROM database.

F3—PRINT: 1. This allows you to print the single article reference which is numbered and highlighted. 2. If the full text summary, or abstract is available, pressing this key will provide you with several print options from which to choose. 3. You may also activate this key to print the Subject Guide, Help Screens, or the Menu.

F5—SUBJECT GUIDE: Allows you to browse through the alphabetical list of subjects and related terms.

F6—BACK-TRAC: Allows you to go back to the previous steps in your search. Takes you from the HELP screen back to your search.

E—EXPANDED SEARCH: Allows you to expand or modify the search (e.g. add search terms) [located on alphabetic keyboard].

Esc—ESCAPE: Allows you to return to a previous screen (or step in your search).

TO SEARCH

At the introductory screen, type your subject headings and press SEARCH/ENTER. If a match is not found, "See" references are given. "See also" references can also determine appropriate search terms. "See also" references will be listed first with subheadings following.

For example, type: TAX REFORM and press SEARCH/ENTER. The screen for TAX REFORM would look like this:

```
> TAX REFORM
    see also
        ALTERNATIVE MINIMUM TAX
        CORPORATE MINIMUM TAX
        FLAT-RATE INCOME TAX
    - ADDRESSES, ESSAYS, LECTURES
    - AIMS AND OBJECTIVES
    - ANALYSIS
    - ANECDOTES, FACETIAE, SATIRE, ETC.
    - ANNIVERSARIES, ETC.
    - BOOKS
    - BUSINESS APPLICATIONS
```

Next, browse the subject guide using the movement, or arrow, keys. Choose the subheading you want with the arrow keys. The search term chosen will be highlighted. Then press the SEARCH/ENTER key. An additional screen will display the bibliographic references. For example, if you chose "Addresses, essays, lectures," the screen would look like this:

```
        REFERENCES: 1 OF 7
    - Congress and the work place; tax reform and employee benefits. (Frank
        B. McArdle speech) (transcript) Vital Speeches Jan. 15'87 p215(5)
```

To browse citations, press NEXT LINE [↓] or PRIOR LINE [↑].

To select subject, press [←].

HOW TO EXPAND OR MODIFY THE SEARCH

The following are the major features making up the Expanded Search Option:

1. Combine terms or concepts: This feature allows you to narrow the search and get more directly relevant citations—without having to browse a large number of headings or citations. The ANDing function is done for you automatically.

2. Search keywords: With this feature, you can search using words that are not standard Library of Congress subject headings. You are likely to get more "hits" because the search is now expanded to include words occurring in the article title and its annotation, as well as the LC headings and subheadings.

3. View the list of headings used to index each article. When you find a citation that is particularly relevant to your topic—use this feature to display the headings used for indexing that article. Then, get a listing of all other citations appearing under each of those headings. Now you know the appropraite LC heading to use for your topic.

For example, to search for the topic "the link between fluoride and cancer":

1. Begin by entering "fluoride and cancer":   Since there is no exact match in the SUBJECT GUIDE, you will be taken to the term "fluorides." You may now browse the list of subheadings for one that might contain references discussing cancer, or press E to implement the Expanded Search function.

2. After pressing E, your original entry will appear on the screen ("fluoride and cancer"):   You may modify it by adding or deleting terms or press the SEARCH/ENTER key to begin the Expanded Search. Note: you may omit words like "and" and other prepositions as these will not be searched. Enter your topic this way: "fluoride cancer."

3. In the Expanded Search mode: The InfoTrac system now searches for all occurrences of the terms "fluoride" and "cancer" in the subject heading, subheading, title, and title annotation fields and then retrieves only those citations which include both those words—i.e. both the ANDing and keyword searching features are being implemented.

4. Citations list: A message indicating the number of citations found appears. You may then retrieve, print, or download any or all citations.

5. Each citation includes one of the following messages:
    a. Headings Available   (can view subject terms assigned to the article)
    b. Headings/Abs Available   (can view subject terms and/or an abstract)
    c. Headings/Text Available   (can view subject terms and/or text of article)
    d. More Information Available   (can view headings, abstract, and text)

Move the highlight bar to the appropriate citation, press SEARCH/ENTER and follow the onscreen instructions.

ANSWERS TO PRACTICE QUESTIONS

1. Search: Basic Instinct

   This search will lead you to:

   > Basic Instinct
   >
   > – (movie reviews)

   Choose this by pressing SEARCH/ENTER—this will give you a list of movie review citations.

2. Search: carjacking

   There is no exact match for this term. Use the Expanded search with this term to get a list of citations. One of the references will look like this:

   Carjacking bill roars through; other crime bills still in park. by Kitty Dumas il v50 *Congressional Quarterly Weekly Report* Oct 10 '92 p3167(1)

   HEADINGS & ABSTRACT AVAILABLE

3. Search: Computer Crimes

   Highlight the subheading *case studies.* Choose this by pressing SEARCH/ENTER—this will give you a list of articles about this topic.

4. Search: Perot, Ross

   The screen will look like this:

   > Perot, Ross
   >
   > See Perot, H. Ross

   Highlight the *see* reference. The screen will list *Perot, H. Ross* and numerous subheadings. Choose the subheading *Economic Policy* to get a list of citations.

5. If you aren't sure of the appropriate subject heading, Search: Stereos

   With the subject list that comes up on the screen, you can then either browse the subject headings or use Expanded Search. If you use the Expanded Search option, a number of citations will come up with the term *Stereos.* You may want to then determine the appropriate subject heading by choosing a citation and highlighting *Check Related Headings.* This will lead you to the subject heading *Stereo Systems.* When you search: Stereo Systems, you will see the subheading *Evaluation.* Choose this for a list of appropriate citations.

6. Search: Somalia

   Choose the subheading *Famines* which will give you a list of citations in reverse chronological order.

7. If you aren't sure of the appropriate subject heading, Search: Models and Eating

   There is no match for this search. Try an Expanded Search and this will give you a few references about this topic.

8. Search: Jackson, Michael

   Choose the subheading *Biography* for a list of citations.

9. Search: Kitchen God's Wife

   This will lead you to a list of citations for book reviews.

10. Search: AIDS

    The screen will look like this:

    AIDS

    　　　See AIDS (disease)

    Highlight the *See* reference and press SEARCH/ENTER. This search will list a number of *See also* references, including:

    See also AIDS (disease) in children

    Highlight this *See also* reference and press SEARCH/ENTER. Choose the subheading *Care and Treatment* for a list of references on this topic.

InfoTrac Training Module adapted from: *Using InfoTrac.* Foster City, CA: Information Access Company, 1993.

TRAINING TIPS

- Several days before the *PsycLit* training, encourage the paraprofessional to pay special attention to reference interviews that involve using *PsycLit*.

- For the training session, start at the computer and explain to the paraprofessional how to use your equipment—booting; rebooting; menu choices; network protocols; etc.

- Then explain the concept of descriptors, use of dashes, use of the asterisk, use of *Thesaurus* (print or online depending on your library's general practice) and keyboard commands.

- Have several searches ready for the paraprofessional to try as examples.

- Make sure the paraprofessional understands how to read the citations on the screen and understands the connection between the citations and your collection—periodical lists or the library catalog.

- Have the paraprofessional do the practice questions and read the handout as a review. If your library has prepared handouts for patrons, use these instead of preparing a new handout. In this way, the paraprofessional learns what information the patrons are seeing.

Module 4: PsycLit Training

OBJECTIVES

1. Given a subject, locate the correct term to use on *PsycLit* according to the *Thesaurus of Psychological Index Terms*.

2. Using any resources available, correctly use the Boolean concepts, AND and OR.

3. Using any resources available, correctly use *PsycLit* 90 percent of the time to answers questions related to psychology.

PRACTICE QUESTIONS

Using the most recent *PsycLit* disk available, do each search in the articles and book chapters section of the database. These questions are to give you practice using the CD-ROM and the *Thesaurus*. Your search strategies may be different than the ones I have supplied in the answers. If there was a real patron asking the question, you would have an opportunity to gain a complete understanding of the question.

1. I am looking for information about Jean Piaget.

2. I am studying ways of helping people deal with grief. I am wondering what has been done with art therapy for grief stricken people.

3. I need information about the language of mentally retarded people.

4. Is there any information about professional ethics in child psychiatry?

5. I want to know what research has been done about what happens to kids who see lots of violence on television.

6. Is there any way to tell if a person in a job interview will be a good employee?

7. I am in charge of motivating the sales force at my company. Can you give me any suggestions?

PSYCLIT TRAINING HANDOUT

PsycLit is a CD-ROM that indexes articles and book chapters related to psychology. The indexing of periodical articles is the same as *Psychological Abstracts*. The library owns two disks, one covering 1987 to the present and one covering 1974 to 1986. The reference staff will change the disks for patrons if they want to search the earlier years.

Every article or book chapter that is indexed is assigned a group of "descriptors," words or phrases that describe what the article discusses. When you search *PsycLit*, you can search through the descriptors to find all of the articles that deal with the subjects in which you are interested. Then you can tell *PsycLit* to combine your subjects to identify articles that talk about how your subjects overlap or connect. Here's how you proceed:

- First you must decide if you want to search for articles or book chapters.
- Highlight your choice using the up and down arrow keys.
- Press the space bar. A check mark should appear next to your choice.
- Press <enter>
- Wait a few minutes.

Let's say you would like to know about drug abuse among teenagers. You should use the *Thesaurus of Psychological Index Terms* to identify the correct subject headings for each of your subjects. When you look up "teenagers," you will see a note saying: "USE Adolescents." To do a thorough *PsycLit* search about teenagers you must use this phrase.

Next you should use the *Thesaurus* to look for drug abuse as a subject. This time we see DRUG ABUSE in bold print. This indicates it is an acceptable subject heading or descriptor. Notice the information beneath DRUG ABUSE. These are other descriptors that you might want to use—DRUG USAGE, ALCOHOL ABUSE, DRUG DEPENDENCY, ADDICTION. Notice the letters in the left hand column next to these words, they indicate the relationship of the term to DRUG ABUSE:

- B is for broader terms—DRUG USAGE includes many concepts, including DRUG ABUSE
- N is for narrower terms —ALCOHOL ABUSE, DRUG DEPENDENCY, and INHALANT ABUSE are examples of, or narrower ideas than, DRUG ABUSE
- R is for related terms—ADDICTION, DRUG OVERDOSES are terms related to DRUG ABUSE but not broader or narrower (you may wish to tell the trainee something such as "When you are more familiar with *PsycLit* and the idea of descriptors, I will show you how to use the *Thesaurus* on the CD-ROM".)
- You can tell *PsycLit* to find all of the articles about teenagers.

    find: adolescents-

When you enter a one word descriptor, you need to put a hyphen at the end of the word. *PsycLit* responds that there are 3288 articles in the system that have "adolescents" as a descriptor. This does not mean these articles talk about teenagers and drug abuse. The articles could discuss any aspect of adolescent life.

Next we have *PsycLit* find all of the articles that discuss drug abuse:

find: drug-abuse

PsycLit expects you to enter multiple word phrases with hyphens between the words: drug-abuse. *PsycLit* indicates there are 2,509 articles that talk about drug abuse. Again, all of these articles are not specifically about adolescent drug abuse.

Notice that each time you enter a search, *PsycLit* gives it a number in the far left column. After entering a search term, you should refer to it by its number rather than retyping the term. Now we tell *PsycLit* to put the two groups together:

find: #1 and #2

There are 135 articles that discuss drug abuse among teenagers.

PsycLit looked at the descriptors of all the articles that discussed adolescents to see which ones also listed drug abuse. The AND command on PsycLit means that both terms—in this case, adolescents and drug abuse—have to be assigned to an article for it to be retrieved. If only one of the phrases is used in the descriptor list for an article, that article will not be selected.

Let's say we are interested in the drug abuse of teenagers or women. We check the *Thesaurus* to learn that for women, we need to use the phrase HUMAN FEMALES. Now we have *PsycLit* search for articles that have been assigned the descriptor human-females:

find: human-females

PsycLit responds that there are 3,474 articles. We combine these with the articles about teenagers:

find: #4 or #1

All of these articles talk about adolescents or women. The OR command on *PsycLit* means either of the selected terms must be in the descriptor field for the article to be selected.

When we combine this set with the set of articles that discuss drug abuse:

find: #2 and #5

We learn that there are 181 articles that discuss drug abuse among women or teenagers. To display records:

Press [F4]

On the most recent disk, you can search either articles or book chapters but you can search only one type of material at a time. To switch sections and do exactly the same search again:

- Press [F8]
- Press [F8] again
- Highlight the section of the database you want to use
- Press [space bar]
- Press <enter>
- Enter the set number you want to have searched: #6 <enter>

You do not need to retype your search terms, just refer to them by the set number *PsycLit* gave it in the left hand column.

8. My company wants to start offering courses to help people deal with job-related stress. Do you think *PsycLit* will help?

9. I think eating habits are affected by the television shows and commercials people see. Have any studies been done about this?

10. My professor thinks I should write a paper about how often black people vote and why they do or don't vote. Where can I find some information?

ANSWERS TO PRACTICE QUESTIONS

All of these answers are set up as if each question is a separate search. For your set numbers to match those given here, you will need to clear the screen after every search. To clear the screen, press the F10 key, then the "C" key. *PsycLit* will respond "CLEAR:" Type "end" and press <enter>.

1. Jean Piaget is the subject of 158 articles and 142 book chapters if you use the following search:

    find: piaget-jean

2. After checking the *Thesaurus*, you know that both art therapy and grief are descriptors. This search should result in six articles and two book chapters:

    find: art-therapy

    find: grief-

    find: #1 and #2

3. You should be able to locate two articles and two book chapters using this search strategy:

    find: language-

    find: mental-retardation

    find: #1 and #2

4. There are four articles and five book chapters on *PsycLit* using the search:

    find: professional-ethics

find: child-psychiatry

find: #1 and #2

5. You should find eight articles and five book chapters that discuss television violence and children if you use this search:

find: (television- or television-viewing)

find: violence-

find: children-

find: #3 and #4 and #5

6. This one needs some reinterpreting. If you can get the patron to tell you more, you will have better luck finding descriptors to use. A good guess would be that what the patron wants is along the lines of the search below, which results in 19 articles but no book chapters:

find: (job-screening or job-applicant-screening or job-applicants)

find: occupational-success-prediction

find #4 and #5

7. *PsycLit* has one article and zero book chapters using this search:

find: motivation-

find: sales-personnel

find: #1 and #2

8. This might take some searching in the *Thesaurus* to locate search terms that will describe the request. Eleven articles and six book chapters are available using this search:

find: employee-assistance-programs

find: occupational-stress

find: #1 and #2

9. Looking through the *Thesaurus* is important for this one. By using television-* rather than television-, we will get all of the descriptors that have the word television in the descriptor field, including television and television advertising. But for food, we really only want articles that talk specifically about food or food preferences, so we will use food- or food-preferences. This search should get five articles and one book chapter:

> find: television-*
>
> find: (food- or food-preferences)
>
> find: #1 and #4

10. You should be able to locate eight articles and one book chapter that might be helpful:

> find: voting-behavior
>
> find: blacks
>
> find: #1 and #2

TRAINING TIPS

Book reviews here are used as an example of a genre training module. Your library may have more questions about other groups of sources such as movie or product reviews.

- Have the paraprofessional read the handout.

- Meet with the paraprofessional to review the sources. Help him or her find where periodical abbreviations are defined in *Book Review Index*.

- Spend time explaining the citation style and use of word counts in *Book Review Digest*. Point out the subject index in *Book Review Digest* if this is useful to your patrons.

- Help the paraprofessional locate the "Book Review" section in the back of H.W. Wilson Company indexes.

- If you use *New York Times* or *Readers' Guide* for review citations, discuss how their arrangement differs from the other book reviewing sources.

- Make sure the paraprofessional understands the connection between the indexes and your collection.

- Have the paraprofessional complete the practice questions.

Module 5: Book Review Training

OBJECTIVES

1. Using any resources available, identify the library's book reviewing sources.

2. Using any resources available, identify the library's sources for locating bibliographic information about books.

3. Using any resources available, locate a review of a non-fiction or fiction title, if a review has been published, within ten minutes of the reference interview.

PRACTICE QUESTIONS

1. Where can I find a review of Danielle Steele's most recent book?

2. Where was Bill Cosby's 1987 book, *Time Flies,* reviewed?

3. I need a review of the book *Origin of Species.*

4. Did the *New York Times Book Review* print a review of *Shot On Location* by Helen Nielsen in 1971?

5. Where can I find a review of *Women's Work, Men's Work.* I don't want reviews from "librarian's" magazines.

6. Is there any easy way to tell if reviewers liked the book, *Machines with a Purpose* by H.H. Rosenbrock?

7. Can I find any reviews of Susan Jeffers' illustrations of the children's book *Brother Eagle, Sister Sky?*

ANSWERS TO PRACTICE QUESTIONS

1. If Danielle Steele's most recent book was published in the last month or two, *InfoTrac* will probably indicate where to find reviews of the book. If the book has been out longer than a few months, then check *Book Review Index* or *Book Review Digest*.

BOOK REVIEW TRAINING HANDOUT

Book reviews are usually printed in newspapers or magazines. Therefore, special indexes to these periodical sources can be consulted to identify the issues of the journals that reviewed the book in which you are interested.

When looking for book reviews, the author's name, book title, and publication year are needed. A review of the book will more likely be located if you have at least two of these pieces of information. There are many more books published every year than get reviewed, so you may end up not finding book reviews more often than you locate reviews.

Book review indexing sources are typically divided chronologically. Therefore, it is necessary to have a basic idea about the book's publication date. Because reviewing sources are also generally arranged by author, it is helpful to know the author's name. Knowing the title is useful especially when the author has a common name or has written more than one book.

If any piece of information is missing, consult the bibliographic sources listed below. One of them may have a full citation to the book and thus provide the information needed to locate a book review.

1. Library catalog to see if the library owns the title.
2. *Books in Print* (New York: R R Bowker. ISSN: 0068-0214). Annual. Provides purchasing information for English-language books that are currently available to buy.
3. *Cumulative Book Index* (New York: H W Wilson. ISSN: 0011-300x). Eleven/year. Provides cataloging information for books published during a given year.
4. *Publishers Trade List Annual* (New York: R R Bowker. ISSN: 0079-7855). Annual. Reprints the catalogs of self-selected publishers.
5. *OCLC* (Dublin, OH: OCLC, Inc. Online bibliographic utility). Provides bibliographic information for more than 20 million items available from more than 12,000 libraries throughout the world.

The best places to start looking for reviews are:

1. *Book Review Digest* (New York: H W Wilson. ISSN: 0006-7326, monthly except February and July). Gives a short excerpt from book reviews published in more than 100 periodicals. In addition to the excerpts, citations to complete reviews are given. An author and title index that covers 1905-1974 is available. For books published before 1974, search by author or title in this index to determine which year(s) to check in the *Digest* for citations to the needed reviews.

2. *Book Review Index* (Detroit: Gale Research, Inc. ISSN: 0524-0581, bimonthly). Index to book reviews published in more than 500 periodicals. Gives a citation to the review(s).

To locate reviews in either source, use the volume for the year of the book's publication and one or two years after publication. (There is really no way to know exactly when the book might have been reviewed, even if the publication date is known). Both the *Index* and *Digest* are arranged by author.

Another good source is the book review section of the indexes published by the H.W. Wilson Company. Choose the subject that should apply:

1. *General Science Index* (New York: H.W. Wilson. ISSN: 0162-1963, monthly except June and December). Useful for books about earth science, chemistry, environment, mathematics, zoology, biology, botany, and other related fields.
2. *Biological and Agricultural Index* (New York: H.W. Wilson. ISSN: 0006-3177, monthly except August).
3. *Education Index* (New York: H.W. Wilson. ISSN: 0013-1385, monthly September-June). Useful for books about education.

To locate reviews in H.W. Wilson Company subject indexes, first find the years needed. Turn to the back of the volume to the section labeled "Book Reviews." Citations to reviews are arranged alphabetically by the book author's last name. This will lead the patron to a magazine in which a review appeared.

Often indexes to general magazines or newspapers can be useful places to search for book reviews as well. You might want to check:

1. *InfoTrac: General Periodicals Index* (Foster Park, CA: Information Access Company. ISSN: 1064-8399). Enter the title of the book as a search. A list of citations to reviews should appear.
2. *Readers' Guide to Periodical Literature.* (New York: H.W. Wilson Company. ISSN: 0034-0464). Turn to the back of the index to the section labeled "Book Review." Look for the name of the author of the book.

2. Either *Book Review Index* or *Book Review Digest* for 1987 will include citations to reviews of Cosby's book.

3. Here we need to turn to the author/title index of *Book Review Digest* to see who wrote *Origin of Species* and when it might have been reviewed. This indicates the 1960 volume will contain reviews of Charles Darwin's book.

4. Taking a look at the periodicals indexed by *Book Review Index* indicates it did cover *New York Times Book Review* in 1971. Simply turn to "Nielsen, Helen" in the 1971 volume for a citation to a review in *New York Times Book Review*.

5. After consulting the library catalog, *Books in Print*, or other bibliographic sources to learn that *Women's Work, Men's Work* was published in 1986, we can begin the search for reviews. H.W. Wilson Company indexes for subject areas provide citations to reviews of books from journals within that specialty. In this case, both *Business Periodicals Index* 1986-1987 and *Social Sciences Index* 1987-1988 cite reviews of the book in question.

6. First you need to determine when Rosenbrock published his book using any of the bibliographic sources. After you learn it was in 1990, then the place to start is *Book Review Digest* because it will give brief excerpts of the review that should give the patron some sense of reaction to the book without having to read the whole review.

7. Using *Book Review Digest* may be easiest here because the digests of the reviews will generally indicate if the author commented on the illustrations or just the story content. Citations to reviews will also be included in *Book Review Index*, but the patron will need to read the review to see if the reviewer commented on the art.

TRAINING TIPS

- Meet with the paraprofessional and use the handout as a review tool.

- Explain to the paraprofessional why most of your patrons seek business information—job seekers, businessmen doing research, students preparing assignments, etc.

- Explain the concepts of public and private companies, international and domestic companies, and parents and subsidiaries. Explain how these different categories of institutions affect the information available about them. Show a sample directory entry to demonstrate that information can be quite scarce.

- Explain the use of Standard Industrial Classification (SIC) codes.

- Emphasize that periodical articles are a very useful source for most non-directory type information.

- Ask the paraprofessional to identify the differences between the directory sources (*Million Dollar Directory, Standard and Poor's Register of Corporations, Ward's*).

- Have the paraprofessional answer the practice questions and review the answers with him or her.

MODULE 6:
Business Sources Training

OBJECTIVES

1. Using any available resources, locate directory information about United States companies.

2. Using any available sources, locate information about industries.

3. Using any available resources, correctly answer 75 percent of requests for company addresses or information about company activities five minutes after completion of a reference interview.

PRACTICE QUESTIONS

1. I need information about Burger King's advertising campaign.

2. Where can I find a list of the top five clothing stores in the United States?

3. I need a list of hardware stores in the United States, with addresses and names of the top executives.

4. Where are current statistics about companies that sell vending machines?

5. Where can I find stock information about the National Pizza Co.?

6. I need to know who in Ohio makes humidity indicators.

7. I need to get a history of the Nestle Company.

8. Where can I get sales figures for Adolph Coors Co.?

9. I need a copy of the Black & Decker logo.

10. Have there been any predictions for personal computer sales and production for the next five to ten years?

ANSWERS TO PRACTICE QUESTIONS

1. Check in *Business Periodicals Index,* or *The Wall Street Journal Index* under the subject heading "Burger King Corporation."

2. First, look in the *Standard Industrial Classification Manual* under "clothing stores, family—retail." Here you will find that the SIC code is 5651. Then, a good source to use to answer this question is *Ward's Business Directory of U.S. Private and Public Companies* under the SIC code 5651.

3. Consult the *Standard Industrial Classification Manual* under "hardware stores—retail." The SIC code is 5251. Then there are a few possibilities. The *Million Dollar Directory* "Series Cross Reference by Industry" volume under SIC 5251 gives company names and addresses. Alphabetic volumes would then have to be consulted for names of chief officers. *Standard & Poor's Register of Corporations, Directors, & Executives* SIC index will give the patron a list of hardware stores; he or she will then have to consult volume 1, the alphabetic index, for addresses and names of chief officers.

4. This one may take some searching. *Business Periodicals Index,* or *The Wall Street Journal Index* under "Vending Machines Industry—Statistics" may lead to some journal articles about the industry.

5. *Standard and Poor's Stock Reports: Over-the-Counter & Regional Exchanges* includes National Pizza Company. If the most recent information is needed, the patron would have to check in the most recent issues of the *Wall Street Journal* (New York: Dow Jones. ISSN 0163-089x or 0043-0080; daily, except Saturday and Sunday).

6. *Thomas Register of American Manufacturers* "Products and Services" volume under "Indicators, Humidity" lists producers by state.

7. You can check the library's subject catalog under "Nestle Company." *Everybody's Business* happens to include Nestle. Another option would be to use *Business Periodicals Index,* or *Wall Street Journal Index* for a reference to an article that could be helpful. Look under the company name.

8. Check the index of *Standard & Poor's Corporation Records* or the *Million Dollar Directory* under "Coors." This should direct the patron to the entry about Coors, which should include sales data.

BUSINESS SOURCES TRAINING HANDOUT

DIRECTORIES

Million Dollar Directory. (Parsippany, NJ: Dun and Bradstreet, Inc. ISSN: 0734-2861). Annual. Directory information about private and public companies. Can provide sales, number of employees, description of business, officers and directors, and company logo. Listed alphabetically by company name, location, and type of industry.

Standard and Poor's Register of Corporations, Directors and Executives. (New York: Standard and Poor's Corporation. ISSN: 0361-3623). Annual. Directory information including: officers and directors' names, description of business, sales, number of employees, and division names and functions. Sometimes includes company logo. Arranged in alphabetical order by company name. Indexed by SIC, location, subsidiary/parent company, and individuals. Includes an obituary index for corporate officers listed in previous editions.

Thomas Register of American Manufacturers. (New York: Thomas Publishing. ISSN: 0362-7721). Annual. Three different sections: "Products and Services" volumes give an alphabetical list of products and services of U.S. companies arranged by state and then city. Provides company names, addresses, brand names, phone numbers, and sales for each company. "Catalogs" volumes provide catalogs for some of the companies included in "Products and Services" section. Volumes labeled "Company Profiles" give company name, address, sales, and phone number. "Catalogs" and "Company Profiles" are arranged alphabetically. A trademark index is also included, which provides an alphabetical list of trademarks reported to Thomas by companies listed in the set.

Ward's Business Directory of US Private and Public Companies. (Detroit, MI: Gale Research. ISSN: 0882-7990). Annual. Directory information including financial data and names of officers for domestic and foreign private and public companies. Arranged alphabetically by company name, with geographic indexes and ranks by sales.

INDEXES

As with all indexes, you may need to check several years worth of indexes before finding information on your particular subject.

Business Periodicals Index. (New York: H W Wilson. ISSN: 0007-6961). Quarterly. Indexes approximately 300 business magazines. Can search by company name (e.g. State Farm Mutual Automobile Insurance Co.) or industry (e.g. health care industry). Updated monthly and alphabetized by subject.

The Wall Street Journal Index. (Ann Arbor, MI: UMI. ISSN 0099-9660). Monthly. Indexes and provides brief abstracts of articles appearing in *The Wall Street Journal.* There is one index for stories about companies and another "General News" index.

Standard Industrial Classification Manual. (Springfield, VA: National Technical Information Service. GPO Order no. PB 87-100012.) Irregular. Provides Standard Industrial Classification number for all United States industries. Used in locating information in other sources which are arranged by SIC. Indexed by subject.

COMPANY INFORMATION

Standard & Poor's Corporation Records. (New York: Standard and Poor's. ISSN: 0196-4674.) Loose-leaf, daily. Good for a brief description of a particular company and relatively current financial information as well as a list of subsidiaries. Alphabetic index is in the front of the volume.

Stock Reports. (New York: Standard and Poor's Corporation. New York Stock Exchange, ISSN: 0160-4899; American Stock Exchange, ISSN: 0191-1112; Over-the-Counter, ISSN: 0163-1993). Quarterly. Current and retrospective information on companies traded on the New York, American, and Over-the-Counter stock exchanges. It is updated weekly. To locate a company, it is necessary to know its stock exchange. Use the index in the "A" volume to find the page number for the company you are researching.

Everybody's Business. edited by Milton Moskowitz, Robert Levering, and Michael Katz. (New York: Doubleday, 1990. ISBN: 0-385-26547-6). Brief descriptions of approximately 400 companies including their history and statistics about number of employees; sales; and profits.

INDUSTRY INFORMATION

Standard & Poor's Industry Surveys. (New York: Standard and Poor's Corporation. ISSN 0196-4666). Quarterly. Includes both narrative and statistics describing the current situation, recent developments, and prospects for many industries. Indexed by company name and product.

United States Industrial Outlook. (Washington, DC: US Department of Commerce. ISSN: 0748-2671). Annual. Narrative description and statistical information about 350 United States industries. Arranged by industry with subject index.

9. *Everybody's Business* and *Standard and Poor's Register of Corporations* include a copy of the logo.

10. *US Industrial Outlook* may provide some information and *Standard and Poor's Industry Surveys* has a section on "Computers." Any of the periodical indexes might lead to magazine or newspaper articles that would include predictions for the computer industry.

Business Sources Training Module adapted from Judith K. Ohles. *Training Coordinator's Manual: A Handbook for Training Preprofessionals at a Reference Desk.* Kent, OH: Kent State University. (ERIC ED 301 221). 1988.

TRAINING TIPS

- Have the paraprofessional read the handout. Meet with him or her and point out that recent information is often difficult to find because libraries depend on indexes which are, by their nature, not current.

- Help the paraprofessional identify regular columns or sections in your local paper and other daily and weekly periodicals you receive that provide succinct current information—"World Happenings" type features.

- Encourage the paraprofessional to stay abreast of the news.

- Remind the paraprofessional that patrons definition of "recent" or "last week" is often faulty and should generally be taken with a grain of salt.

- Have the paraprofessional complete the practice questions and review the answers with him or her.

- Pick one or two recent events (one, two or three weeks old and another two or three months old) and as you introduce each source to the paraprofessional , have him or her look for information about the event. Compare the amount of information provided by each type of source—periodicals vs. indexes.

MODULE 7: Current Events Training

OBJECTIVES FOR CURRENT EVENTS TRAINING SESSION

1. From memory, identify the most current indexing sources available in the library.

2. Using any resources available, correctly answer 90 percent of all requests for information about national and international events that occurred in the past year.

PRACTICE QUESTIONS

1. I'd like information about the recent airplane crash.

2. I want to know how my representative voted on the recent _____ legislation.

3. I need information about Harris Wofford. I think he ran for Senate several years ago.

4. I need some detailed information about congressional activities of last week.

5. Can I find a copy of the speech the President gave last week?

6. Who won the most recent World Series?

7. I understand elections were recently held in the country of _____. Can you tell me who is the president now?

8. Do you have any information about why the stock market fell/rose last week?

9. Who was involved in the terrorist attack that took place last week?

ANSWERS TO PRACTICE QUESTIONS

1. If the crash was very recent, thumbing through issues of magazines and newspapers may be the best source of information. Recent articles on this may be identified by using *Readers' Guide to Periodical Literature* or *The New York Times Index* under the subject heading of "Airlines—accidents." It can also be helpful to look under the name of the airline. *Facts on File* will

CURRENT EVENTS TRAINING HANDOUT

PERIODICALS

Newspapers provide the most up-to-date information available. Often if patrons need information about a very current topic, they will have to search through individual issues of newspapers or magazines to find articles about their topic of interest. For topics that are several months old, patrons can begin their search in indexes, which are discussed below.

Many magazines come out each week and can give you information about a current event. To learn about all of the periodicals the library receives each week, check the periodical holdings list of the library. Keep in mind that often magazines are post-dated. When looking for a magazine with information about an event that took place on September 1, you may need to check the September 15 issues. (This is because the periodical published on September 1 is dated September 7. Information about a September 1 event would not be included until the issue distributed on September 7, which will be dated September 15).

Newsweek. (New York: Newsweek. ISSN: 0028-9604). Weekly.

Time. (New York: Time Inc. ISSN: 0040-781X). Weekly.

U.S. News & World Report. (Washington, DC: U.S. News & World Report. ISSN: 0041-5537). Weekly. Three popular periodicals that contain sections about national, international, and business events.

Business Week. (New York: McGraw-Hill Inc. ISSN: 0007-7135). Weekly. A popular business magazine that includes information from a business perspective about current events; includes articles about international events and U.S. government activities.

Sports Illustrated. (New York: Time Inc. ISSN: 0038-822X). Weekly. A weekly look at sports, including amateur, collegiate, and professional athletes and teams.

Congressional Quarterly Weekly Report. (Washington, DC: Congressional Quarterly, Inc. ISSN: 0010-5910). Weekly. Gives detailed reports on government activities. Covers bills, acts, how members of Congress voted, major legislation, and related subjects. Also lists lobbyists who have registered with the House of Representatives and legislation of interest to them. Subject index is updated weekly.

Facts on File. (New York: Facts on File. ISSN:0014-6641). Weekly. Provides a paragraph or two about many current topics. International in scope, but emphasizes important events that have occurred in the United States. Gives texts of major political speeches. A detailed index is issued every two weeks with quarterly and annual cumulations. A cumulative index is issued every five years.

Current Biography. (Bronx, New York: HW Wilson. ISSN: 0011-3344). Monthly except December. Biographical sketches of international personalities, with references listed. Always includes a photograph. Includes entertainers, writers, athletes, politicians, and researchers. Cumulative index for 1940-1985; 1981-89. Most recent paperback edition has cumulative index for the year.

INDEXES

Indexes provide listings of magazine and newspaper articles on current topics. They are often updated monthly, and therefore may be useful for locating information about recent events.

Readers' Guide to Periodical Literature. (New York: H.W. Wilson Company. ISSN: 0034-0464). Seventeen issues per year. Alphabetical index to articles from more than 200 general interest magazines.

The New York Times Index. (New York: The New York Times Company. ISSN: 0147-538X). Semi-monthly. Indexes and provides brief abstracts of articles that appeared in *The New York Times.*

InfoTrac: General Periodicals Index. (Foster City, CA: Information Access Company. ISSN: 1064-8399). A CD-ROM index with some abstracts for 1100 general interest magazines.

provide brief information under the subject heading "Accidents—aviation."

2. *Congressional Quarterly Weekly Report* will tell you how all Senators and Representatives voted on all of the bills and resolutions in any session. Check the index under the subject areas the patron wants (e.g., if the legislation in question dealt with agriculture, look in the index under "agriculture"). The entry there will lead you to the page that has a chart indicating how everyone voted.

3. Just our luck, *Current Biography* published a biography of Harris Wofford in 1992. If further information is needed, the patron could use the list of references at the end of the article. *Readers' Guide to Periodical Literature* and *The New York Times Index* might lead to other articles written about him.

4. *Congressional Quarterly Weekly Report* would give detailed coverage. Some of our current magazines and newspapers might also have information about some of the activities of Congress; these sources will tend to focus on big topics or debates.

5. *Congressional Quarterly Weekly Report* is the place to look. Try the index under "Presidential Messages (texts)" to locate the page reference needed. A synopsis may be all that can be located for minor speeches. The text of major speeches, including the State of the Union address, are printed in *Congressional Quarterly Weekly Report*.

6. Depending on how long after October you need to find the name of the winners of the World Series, you may be able to use recent issues of magazines, particularly *Sports Illustrated*. Otherwise, refer to *Facts on File* under "Baseball" or periodical indexes such as *Readers' Guide to Periodical Literature* or *The New York Times Index*.

7. Very recent election results should have been reported in newspapers, magazines, or *Facts on File*. Elections held several months ago will send you to indexes such as *The New York Times Index* or *Readers' Guide to Periodical Literature*. For the *Times Index*, it is probably easiest to look under "Elections" and then search

for the name of the country. You will be given a date. Turn to the entry for the country and look for articles appearing on the date given under the "Elections" entry. In *Readers' Guide*, simply look under "Elections" and then for your country as a subdivision.

8. To locate up-to-date information about the activities of the stock market, *Business Week* may be the best source. Other newspapers and magazines may provide some information, especially if the drop or rise was dramatic.

9. If a terrorist attack really happened last week (it often pays to be skeptical about your patron's memory), current magazines and newspapers will be your best source of information. If the attack took place some time ago, you may need to know the name of the group involved, or the location of the attack to help you find useful subject headings in *Readers' Guide*, *Facts on File*, or *The New York Times Index*. If you do not have complete or accurate information about the name or the location, you can check the above indexes under "Terrorism" and generally find cross references to correct subject headings.

Current Events Training Module adapted from Judith K. Ohles. *Training Coordinator's Manual: A Handbook for Training Preprofessionals at a Reference Desk.* Kent, OH: Kent State University. (ERIC ED 301 221). 1988.

TRAINING TIPS

- Have the paraprofessional read the handout.

- Review with the paraprofessional any ready reference type-information you maintain about local elected officials. Explain the difficulty of getting the correct information immediately after elections.

- Describe the difference between state and federal government; and the judicial, legislative and executive branches of government.

- Discuss why your patrons look for information about the government—personal interest; letter writing; school reports; etc.

- As you review the sources with the paraprofessional, have him or her identify the differences between sources with similar purposes (*Almanac of American Politics* and *Politics in America*; the Congressional Directories or *Congressional Quarterly Almanac* and *Congressional Quarterly Weekly Report*). Make sure the paraprofessional notices the many indexes in the *Weekly Report* and *Almanac*.

- Have the paraprofessional complete the practice questions and review the answers with him or her.

MODULE 8: Government Information Training

OBJECTIVES

1. Using any resources available, identify directories of individuals in government.

2. Using any resources available, identify information sources about government agencies and government activities.

3. Using any resources available, correctly answer 90 percent of all questions about individuals in government, government agencies, and government activities.

PRACTICE QUESTIONS

1. I would like to register a complaint with the SEC. Do you have their phone number?

2. I need information about the Federal Election Commission.

3. Where did Representative William Natcher get his bachelor's degree?

4. I would like information about the Anita Hill/Clarence Thomas hearings.

5. I need the text of President Reagan's AIDS plan presented in 1987.

6. How much money did Ralph Regula raise in his last campaign for re-election?

7. Where can I get a copy of Richard Nixon's resignation speech?

8. I'd like to know how Al Gore and Dan Quayle voted while they were in Congress.

9. Who is currently serving on the Supreme Court?

10. Who are the House and Senate members who have served the longest?

11. Who is the Chairman of the Taskforce on Urgent Fiscal Issues?

ANSWERS TO PRACTICE QUESTIONS

1. Consulting the *Federal Staff Directory* in the "Key Word Subject" index under "Securities and Exchange Commission" refers to the entry where the phone number for complaints or inquiries is provided. Both *The United States Government Manual* and the *Federal Regulatory Directory* give the general phone number.

2. Check the subject index of the *Federal Regulatory Directory* under Federal Election Commission, and you will be referred to an article on the Commission. Short entries are included in the *Encyclopedia of Government Advisory Organizations* and *The United States Government Manual*.

3. Any of the congressional directories should provide this information. The "Name Index" of *Congressional Staff Directory* identifies a biographical sketch, which indicates he received his degree in 1930 from West Kentucky State College.

4. The 1991 *Congressional Quarterly Almanac* gives an overview of the hearings. The *Congressional Quarterly Weekly Reports* for 1991 will provide a weekly review of what occurred, if the patron wants to read through all of the issues. He or she could consult the annual index under "Hill, Anita" or "Thomas, Clarence" for exact page references to the weekly issues that contain information.

   Readers' Guide to Periodical Literature or *InfoTrac* will also provide citations to magazine articles about the hearings. *Facts on File* will also provide some information. You can look under "Hill, Anita" or "Thomas, Clarence" for the exact page numbers to check.

5. There are several choices here. *Congressional Quarterly Almanac* 1987 subject index under "Reagan—health—AIDS" gives the direct page reference. *Congressional Quarterly Weekly Report* 1987 under "AIDS—Reagan Address" also provides the page reference to the text of the speech. You could also consult the "Presidential Texts" index.

6. Either *The Almanac of American Politics* or *Politics in America* will give the information. Look for the entry on Regula and find the chart that details campaign

GOVERNMENT INFORMATION TRAINING HANDOUT

INDIVIDUALS IN GOVERNMENT

The Almanac of American Politics. (Washington DC: National Journal. ISBN: 0-89234-051-7). Annual. Provides a short biographical sketch of all members of Congress and state governors. Also gives statistics on election results and campaign finances. Includes how congress members voted on key issues and how the individual is rated by ten different organizations. Arranged by state with governor and senators first, then representatives arranged by congressional district. Brief essay about political climate in the state. Interfiled name and subject indexes.

Congressional Directory. (Washington, DC: Government Printing Office. ISSN 0160-9890). Annual. Short biographical sketches of members of Congress. Also includes lists of committee members, names and addresses for government departments and agencies, and congressional district maps. Separate subject and name indexes.

Congressional Staff Directory. (Mount Vernon, VA: Congressional Staff Directory. ISBN: 0-87289-086-4). Annual. Directory information about congress members and their staffs. Includes committee assignments. Brief biographies of congress members and their staff members. Indexed by subject and individual.

Politics in America. (Washington, DC: Congressional Quarterly. ISBN: 0-87187-599-3). Annual. Biographical information about all members of Congress, including a one to two page summary of what action the congress member took in the last session. Lists committee assignments, election results, campaign finances, votes on key issues, and rankings by four interest groups. Arranged alphabetically by state; within each state, lists governor, senators, and representatives by Congressional district. Name index.

Federal Staff Directory. (Mount Vernon, VA: Congressional Staff Directory. ISBN: 0-87289-088-0). Annual. Gives name, title, address, and phone number of employees in Executive Departments (agriculture, commerce, defense, etc.) as well as independent agencies. Biographical sketches are provided for key individuals. Indexed by subject and individual.

GOVERNMENT AGENCIES

The United States Government Manual. (Washington DC: Government Printing Office: Office of the Federal Register. ISSN: 0092-1904). Annual. Gives history, description, and mission of federal agencies and names, phone numbers, and addresses of important individuals in each agency. Includes branches of government, agencies, departments, independent establishments, government corporations, boards, committees, commissions, and quasi-official agencies. Indexed by name and agency or subject.

Encyclopedia of Governmental Advisory Organizations. (Detroit, Gale Research Co. ISSN: 0092-8380). Irregular. Gives history, authority, program, staff, membership, publications, and meetings for 5000 advisory organizations. Includes defunct organizations. Arranged by subject with indexes by personnel, department or agency, and keyword.

Federal Regulatory Directory. (Washington DC: Congressional Quarterly, Inc. ISSN: 0195-749x). Quadrennial. For each agency, information about responsibilities, history, powers, authority, biographical information about people on committees, organization, information sources, congressional committees they deal with, legislation that affects their activities, and bibliography of sources for more information. Indexed by name and subject.

INFORMATION ABOUT GOVERNMENT

Congressional Quarterly Weekly Report. (Washington, DC: Congressional Quarterly, Inc. ISSN: 0010-5910). Weekly. Weekly magazine that discusses politics and congressional activities. Short paragraph explanation about every bill voted on with charts indicating how congress members voted. Often reprints texts of presidential speeches and press conferences. Lists registered lobbyists. Subject index every two weeks.

Congressional Quarterly Almanac. (Washington, DC: Congressional Quarterly. Inc., ISSN: 0095-6007). Annual. Reviews congressional action of the past year. Discusses major bills and events of each session of Congress. Special sections deal with decisions of the Supreme Court, key votes of Congress, interest group ratings, texts of presidential speeches, lists of public laws enacted, and charts indicating how every congress member voted on all bills. Arranged by cabinet area (agriculture, treasury, defense, etc.) with a subject index.

Facts on File. (New York: Facts on File. ISSN: 0014-6641). Weekly. Weekly overview of international events. Concentrates on activities concerning the United States. Reprints texts of presidential and political speeches. Indexed first by subject and then chronological. Cumulative index every five years.

InfoTrac: General Periodicals Index. (Foster City, CA: Information Access Company. ISSM: 1064-8399. Identifies articles from more than 1100 magazines that may describe government activities. Search by subject of individual's name.

Readers' Guide to Periodical Literature. (NY: H.W. Wilson Co. ISSN: 0034-0464). Seventeen/year. Indexes many magazines that often include articles dealing with the activities of Congress, the President, and government. Use subject or individual's name as subject heading.

finances. If you need to know specifically about contributions from political action committees (PACs), check *Politics in America.*

7. *Facts on File* 1971-1975 index under "Nixon—Politics—Impeachment and Resignation Issues" indicates when the speech was given and on what page in the 1974 *Facts on File* it can be found.

8. The voting record of Al Gore and Dan Quayle will be recorded in *Congressional Quarterly Almanac* or *Weekly Report.* Charts are provided that show how each congressman voted on each piece of legislation during a particular session of Congress. If you are interested in specific legislation, check the index under that name or topic.

9. The *United States Government Manual* lists the Supreme Court justices. Check the table of contents for the "Judicial Branch" section.

10. *Politics in America* provides a list of Senators and Representatives by party and by seniority, or time served.

11. The Taskforce for Urgent Fiscal Issues is a subgroup of the House Budget Committee. The Taskforce chair is identified in the *Congressional Staff Directory.*

RESOURCES

Bafundo, Donna R. *In-Service Training Program for Library Paraprofessionals: A Report.* Fairfax, VA: George Mason University. June 1981. ERIC ED 207 536. Bafundo describes a seven-module paraprofessional training program that includes introduction to and practice with basic reference sources: business, biographical, indexing and abstracting sources, and government documents.

Creth, Sheila D. *Effective On-the-Job Training: Developing Library Human Resources.* Chicago: American Library Association, 1986. Creth discusses how to develop, implement, and evaluate a training program for all areas of the library.

Hendley, Margaret. "Staff Training in an Automated Environment." *Canadian Library Journal* 46 (April 1989): 101-103. Hendley points out the need for training library staff to work with patrons who are just learning to use an online catalog or CD-ROM. She recommends topics to cover in this type of training and suggests using roleplay, worksheets, and workshops to prepare staff to teach system use.

InfoTrac: General Periodicals Index. Foster City, CA: Information Access Company, 1993.

Ohles, Judith K. *Training Coordinator's Manual: A Handbook for Training Preprofessionals at a Reference Desk.* Kent, OH: Kent State University. (ERIC ED 301 221) 1988. A manual for trainers used at Kent State University Libraries to prepare preprofessionals for reference desk service. Includes training sessions about OCLC, business sources, government documents, legal sources, and current events.

Preece, Barbara G., and Betty J. Glass. "The Online Catalog and Staff Training." *Library Software Review* 10 (March/April 1991): 100-104. Preece and Glass describe the training sessions developed to teach staff at Southern Illinois University at Carbondale to use their new online catalog.

Stanley, Suzanne. "Information Sources." In *Handbook of Library Training Practice,* edited by Ray Prytherch, 207-277. Aldershot, Hants, England: Gower, 1986. Stanley provides examples of training sessions which include reference sources, catalogs, bibliographies, indexes, abstracts, and practice questions; provides objectives and methodologies for broad areas.

Taylor, Margaret T., and Ronald R. Powell. *Basic Reference Sources: A Self-Study Manual.* 3rd ed. Metuchen, NJ: The Scarecrow Press, 1985. Taylor and Powell present a workbook of questions that allow self-paced examination of more than one hundred reference sources. Questions provide guided examination of scope, arrangement, etc., of bibliographies, indexes, biographical sources, encyclopedias, atlases, and dictionaries.

7 PERFORMANCE EVALUATION

Once paraprofessionals have been oriented to the library and trained in their duties, supervisors should begin to evaluate their performance. This evaluation can take several forms, the most obvious being that of a formal evaluation, also known as performance appraisal. Good supervisors also provide their staffs with informal evaluation on an ongoing basis. This method includes both coaching and counseling for job and career development, and providing daily feedback about work performance.

Although as a supervisor you may find performance evaluation difficult, the need for institutions to become more effective and efficient makes evaluation necessary. You need to help the paraprofessionals in your department be responsible for the improvement of their own performance, and thereby improve the overall department's performance. There are several purposes for performance evaluation including improved use of personnel, increased staff development, provision of information about performance to employees, and identification of training needs.

From the viewpoint of the paraprofessionals, formal and informal performance evaluation provides necessary feedback about their work. Employees want to know how they are doing in their jobs and if they are meeting the expectations of their positions.

This chapter will cover coaching and counseling, feedback, formal evaluation, and the performance appraisal interview.

COACHING AND COUNSELING

Coaching and counseling is a management technique that can lead to improved staff morale, an increased commitment to work, and greater levels of staff motivation. Coaching and counseling often involves a meeting between you and the paraprofessional to discuss performance and the job environment. It provides an opportunity for the paraprofessional to identify successes and problems related to job performance. These meetings can be scheduled on a regular basis, bi-monthly or monthly, or farther apart, possibly once every six months. You should have a copy of the job description and a list of all of the tasks or projects that a paraprofessional has been asked to do, and simply go through these one item at a time to hear what has been accomplished and what problems or successes have been encountered.

Coaching and counseling should be handled gently and sensitively. In a coaching and counseling interview pertaining to overall job development, you want paraprofessionals to discuss their work performance and their feelings about work and their place in the organization. The list in Figure 7-1 provides sample questions to ask a paraprofessional in such an interview. It's useful to give the paraprofessional the list about a week before the meeting so that he or she can think about his or her responses.

You should take notes of the responses given and use this information later to compliment or advise the paraprofessional about his or her progress in areas identified as strengths or weaknesses. If the paraprofessional suggests changes in the department that are later implemented, your notes about the suggestion will remind you to give credit to the paraprofessional.

At a follow-up counseling interview, scheduled from three to six months after the initial interview, some of your questions should address changes in work performance since the last session. It is helpful to continue to include questions seven through nine of the previous counseling session (see Figure 7-1) so that paraprofessionals feel that they are a contributing force in the department. This also helps build staff morale and participation, factors that can greatly enhance work performance and job satisfaction. Additional questions that could be asked at a follow-up session are also given in Figure 7-1.

For new paraprofessionals, you may prefer to hold these meetings more frequently, perhaps in three months. For paraprofessionals who have worked at the library longer, coaching and counseling meetings twice a year will be enough to keep the lines of communication open. You may want to point out to paraprofessionals that communication is always welcome; one does not need a scheduled meeting to bring up questions or concerns.

FEEDBACK

Daily feedback is an essential aspect of training, supervising, and evaluating paraprofessionals. Employees need and want feedback because it keeps them informed about your perceptions of their performance. If changes in behavior or attitude are needed, the paraprofessional is made aware of this and given the opportunity to improve. Verbal feedback is especially important for reference

Figure 7-1

COACHING AND COUNSELING

Discussion Questions

1. How do you view yourself and your job in the context of the library, (i.e., what is the special contribution that you make to the smooth functioning of the library)?

2. Discuss areas of your work that warrant recognition, those of which you are most proud. Indicate any plans you may have to maintain and/or strengthen your expertise in these areas.

3. Discuss areas of your work that you feel need strengthening. Indicate any plans you may have to strengthen these areas.

4. Discuss any rewards and joys you have encountered. Indicate ways in which you utilize these rewards to improve your work performance.

5. Discuss any frustrations you have encountered. Indicate ways in which you have dealt with these frustrations. Indicate suggestions you may have for dealing with these frustrations in the future.

6. What do you feel is the most important skill, talent, and/or ability you have to offer? How have you integrated this into your work? How might you further integrate this into your work?

7. Discuss areas of the Reference Department that you feel need strengthening. Indicate any ideas you may have to strengthen these areas.

8. Indicate ways in which service to patrons could be improved.

9. Discuss any other thoughts, feelings, or ideas you have about the Reference Department, your responsibilities and duties, and the library in general.

Follow Up Discussion Questions

1. Which aspects of your job interest you

   a. the most?

   b. the least?

2. Are there any skills you have which your present job does not fully utilize?

3. In what areas do you need training or other help to do your job better?

Figure 7-1   Cont.

4. Where do you see your career going, ideally, in the next five years?

5. In your present job, what sorts of things tell you that you are doing a good job?

6. How could your supervisor help you to do a better and more satisfying job?

   If appropriate, ask:

7. What thoughts do you have about our new service and/or policy (e.g., CD–ROMs, new staffing arrangement)?

From Judith K. Ohles, *Training Coordinator's Manual: A Handbook for Training Preprofessionals at a Reference Desk*. Kent, Ohio: Kent State University. (ERIC ED 301 221). 1988.

staff members since their attitudes and work performance directly affect patrons' attitudes and support of the library. Paraprofessionals need to understand that their work behavior is perceived by patrons as embodiments of the library's philosophies and attitudes. Although both verbal and nonverbal feedback are given in any interaction, emphasize verbal feedback. Nonverbal cues or feedback can be easily misinterpreted.

Immediate feedback is best so that the paraprofessional understands what was done correctly or incorrectly. Generally, feedback should be given in private. When feedback is positive, presenting it in private reinforces its importance. When feedback is negative, privacy is important so that the paraprofessional is not embarrassed and is free to react in anyway he or she feels appropriate.

When providing feedback, it is advisable to focus on job performance and avoid any discussion about the employee's personality. If pointing out a job discrepancy, use actual events or conversations to analyze, with the paraprofessional, the nature and extent of the problem. Do not begin the interview by stating your assumptions; rather ask the paraprofessional to describe the situation or circumstances. Feedback that is viewed as a two-way exchange will allow both you and the paraprofessional to voice any satisfaction or dissatisfaction and can enhance your work relationship. The identification of the problem is perhaps the most important step in such feedback. Once the problem is clearly identified, discuss viable solutions.

There are several communication skills supervisors will want to use when providing or soliciting feedback. For example, it is often useful to paraphrase what the paraprofessional has said in order to clarify his or her concerns and encourage further discussion. Another successful tactic is to reflect the paraprofessional's feeling. For example, you could begin by saying, "I sense that you feel (*emotion*) when (*identify when emotion is demonstrated*)." Then ask for verification, "Is that right?" or "Would you like to talk about it?" To illustrate more completely:

> "Sue, I sense that you feel impatient when a patron without a strong command of English asks a reference question. Is that right?"

Encourage the employee to talk by using nonjudgmental, openended questions. Use closed questions to focus more specifically on a topic or to clarify a certain position. Supervisors who are

WHAT DO YOU THINK?

"Until we read one another's minds, feedback is the only source we have for what others think or feel."

Priscilla DiffieCouch, "How to Give Feedback." In *Performance Evaluation: A Management Basic for Librarians*, ed. Jonathan A. Lindsey (Phoenix: Oryx Press, 1986), 38-41.

willing to work out problems with paraprofessionals are providing the paraprofessionals with opportunities to actively change their work performance.

Another opportunity to meet the paraprofessional in a mutual exchange occurs when an employee is doing exceptionally well in his or her job. Providing positive feedback to employees who consistently perform superbly or who have improved greatly in their jobs will foster enhanced respect for the supervisor, loyalty to the institution, and greater job satisfaction.

Recognize group performance. This can raise staff morale and increase teamwork. For example, if the department as a whole has shown improvement in its public service attitude, it is wise and caring to voice appreciation at a departmental meeting and to inform the higher level supervisor of the change so that he or she realizes the improvement and may compliment the department.

Feedback is an essential component of performance evaluation. Daily feedback decreases the stress of the annual formal evaluation by allowing paraprofessionals to know what is expected of them and how they are doing. Employees should not be surprised by a performance evaluation. If a paraprofessional is not meeting expectations of the job, he or she should know this before a formal evaluation. Continuous feedback, positive or negative, is essential for maintaining employee morale and improving service.

FORMAL EVALUATION

The most prevalent form of performance evaluation is the formal performance appraisal. Usually conducted annually, performance appraisal provides a written record of a paraprofessional's work performance and accomplishments. Basically, appraisals let employees know how they are doing in their jobs and point out areas that need improvement. Most supervisors regard performance appraisal as an important personnel tool that can fill several functions. These include providing concrete feedback, helping employees set goals for themselves, and identifying training needs.

Although formal evaluation is typically administered annually, new paraprofessionals need to be appraised more frequently than senior reference staff. A new paraprofessional often has a probationary period determined by the library. At the end of this period, the paraprofessional will be given his or her first appraisal to determine his or her ability to carry out the requirements of the job.

During the probationary period, you should meet with the paraprofessional to review the job description and how he or she is doing. Paraprofessionals should be aware of when they will be evaluated, and they should be given a copy of the evaluation form during the orientation period. During the meeting to review the job description and evaluation form, the paraprofessional should be permitted to ask about any of the items on the evaluation form. You should be prepared to give an example of excellent and unsatisfactory performance for each category. This is a good opportunity to tell paraprofessionals what they need to do to earn excellent ratings. Every supervisor will want his or her paraprofessionals to be providing the best service possible and should, therefore, be able to distinguish excellent service from satisfactory service.

There are several problems that exist with performance appraisal systems. A good supervisor should be aware of the potential disadvantages and pitfalls of performance appraisal so that they can be avoided.

Each paraprofessional should be evaluated on each task individually. This means the employees should not be compared to one another and that each paraprofessional should be evaluated on his or her ability to do each task. For example, you may have a paraprofessional who works with patrons very well but who generally arrives late for work. In this case, the paraprofessional should receive a high rank for patron interaction and a low rank for punctuality. In this instance, you should not let displeasure with tardiness color your evaluation of other areas of performance, but neither should you let satisfaction with the paraprofessional's work with patrons cause you to overlook performance problems, such as tardiness.

You also need to keep personal feelings out of the performance appraisal process. You should not evaluate performance by how much you or other staff members like the paraprofessional. The evaluation should review all performance since the last evaluation; the evaluation should not focus only on the most recent actions, nor should a paraprofessional continue to be evaluated based on some problem or success that occurred several evaluation periods earlier. It is often useful to use previous evaluations as points of reference, particularly if there has been a drastic change in performance since that time.

It is important to maintain records of employee performance throughout the rating period, noting various aspects of work performance. A review of the training objectives can be useful to see how much the paraprofessional has learned. Notes from coaching and counseling sessions may be used as reminders of past problems or accomplishments that can be mentioned in an evaluation. Letters commenting on the performance of the paraprofessional from patrons or other staff members should be considered as well. You should also review the job description and determine how well the paraprofessional is performing all aspects of the job. And, you should be aware of the seriousness and sensitivity of performance appraisal. Employees have a legal right to know that notes are being kept on their work performance and that they are permitted to see them when requested.

There are a variety of performance appraisal systems, including essay, comparative ranking, management by objectives (MBO), and trait measures. In the course of this manual, we will use only one kind of evaluation system, trait measures, as an example. You will need to consider how all evaluations are done in your library when preparing to evaluate paraprofessionals. In general, all employees in one category should be evaluated using the same type of system.

Trait measures involve rating performance on a scale of five to seven levels of performance (e.g., outstanding, very good, average, marginal, or unsatisfactory). Several different categories of performance are measured, such as results (quantity and quality of work), behavior (relations with others, patron interaction), and individual characteristics (initiative, adaptability). Other factors that can be included are job knowledge, dependability, cooperation, and self-reliance.

Each institution should employ an evaluation form that meets its particular requirements. In large libraries, the personnel office is responsible for creating the form. In smaller libraries, it is often a staff committee that devises the form. The creators of the document first need to decide on the traits, characteristics, and skills that are needed to perform the job satisfactorily. They will also need to choose the number of factors to be evaluated. A sample evaluation form is given in Figure 7-2.

In selecting an applicable list of factors to make up an appraisal system, you need to select aspects of performance that can be rated and are truly relevant to the job. For example, "sense of

HELPFUL SOURCES

Other sources for sample evaluation forms include:

Performance Appraisal (Washington, D.C.: Association of Research Libraries. Systems and Procedures Exchange Center, 1979).

Elizabeth Futas. *The Library Forms Illustrated Handbook* (New York: Neal-Schuman, 1984).

humor" is difficult to rate and probably not a requirement for successful reference work. The rating scale should correspond to the job description.

In addition to selecting traits to evaluate, it can be helpful to provide space for the supervisor to write a paragraph or two about the overall performance of the paraprofessional. This gives you a chance to highlight improvement or special projects completed by the paraprofessional. It is also important to design a form that leaves space for the employee to respond to any part of the evaluation.

PERFORMANCE APPRAISAL INTERVIEWS

No formal evaluation is complete without the performance appraisal interview. You and the paraprofessional must meet to discuss the paraprofessional's evaluation. Both of you can fill out the evaluation form separately and then discuss the areas of agreement and disagreement. The hope here is to reach a consensus about all of the factors rated.

The appraisal interview is perhaps the most important aspect of formal evaluation. This is where the paraprofessional and you have an opportunity to discuss any work performance problems and discuss goals for job improvement. Typically, appraisal interviews are conducted annually. However, if several problems are identified or if the supervisor and the paraprofessional disagree about significant points, a semiannual evaluation and interview should be conducted. Privacy and a lack of interruptions are important to a successful interview. Try to set aside at least one hour for each interview, but to provide a schedule that is flexible enough so that more time can be used if necessary. It is advisable to maintain written records of evaluations and to have both the supervisor and the paraprofessional sign the completed evaluation form at the end of the interview. Paraprofessionals should be informed that the completed form will be added to their personnel file. Encourage them to include written comments of their own on the form.

The many aspects of performance evaluation—coaching and counseling, feedback, formal evaluation—are essential to success-

Figure 7-2

REFERENCE DEPARTMENT EVALUATION FORM

EMPLOYEE_____   PERIOD from _____to_____

Please evaluate the following traits:

	EXCELLENT	VERY GOOD	AVERAGE	BELOW AVG.	UNSATISFA.
1. QUALITY OF WORK (accuracy, neatness, thoroughness)					
2. QUANTITY OF WORK (volume, amount, speed)					
3. STAFF RELATIONSHIPS (works harmoniously with staff at all levels)					
4. ORGANIZATION OF WORK (effective use of time)					
5. KNOWLEDGE OF WORK (understanding, comprehension, knowledge of resources)					
6. JUDGMENT (ability to make decisions, apply knowledge)					
7. INITIATIVE (motivation, interest in work)					
8. ADAPTABILITY (adjusts to changes in work assignments, to uneven work flow)					
9. RELIABILITY (is punctual, adheres to work schedule)					
10. DEPENDABILITY (able to work without direct supervision when necessary, ability to follow through on assignment)					
11. PATRON INTERACTION (displays a visible friendly and helpful attitude towards patrons, is polite and patient)					

COMMENTS: Please include areas of work that warrant special recognition and those that need strengthening (e.g., completion of special projects in an efficient manner, professional demeanor)

COMMENTS BY EMPLOYEE:

DATE: _____

EVALUATOR'S SIGNATURE _____

EMPLOYEE'S SIGNATURE: _____

From Judith K. Ohles. *Training Coordinator's Manual: A Handbook for Training Preprofessionals at a Reference Desk.* Kent, OH: KSU (ERIC ED301221) 1988.

ful management. Performance evaluation fulfills several functions. It provides a basis for personnel and employment decisions, gives feedback to employees and solicits feedback from them, encourages staff development, and determines areas for employee discipline, training, and re-training. Good supervisors need to take advantage of the many opportunities to evaluate paraprofessionals in order to encourage staff morale and maximize the effectiveness of the department's work.

RESOURCES

Gibbs, Sally. "Staff Appraisal" in *Handbook of Library Training Practice*, ed. by Ray Prytherch, 61-81. Hants, England: Gower, 1986. Gibbs argues for the use of performance appraisal in libraries with a discussion of its advantages and disadvantages. Reviews three methods of appraisal and includes sample forms.

Kikoski, John F., and Joseph A. Litterer. "Effective Communication in the Performance Appraisal Interview" in *Performance Evaluation: A Management Basic for Librarians*, edited by Jonathan A. Lindsey, 23-36. Phoenix: Oryx Press, 1986. Kikoski and Litterer review the interpersonal dimensions of performance appraisal and describe the system of microtraining—which includes attentive behaviors, feedback, paraphrasing, reflection of feeling, open and closed questions, and focusing—that appraisers can use to increase the effectiveness of communication during appraisal interviews.

Lindsey, Jonathan A. "The Human Dimension in Performance Appraisal" in *Performance Evaluation: A Management Basic for Librarians*, edited by Jonathan A. Lindsey, 3-8. Phoenix: Oryx Press, 1986. Lindsey provides a review of performance appraisal literature, discusses why performance appraisal sometimes does not work, and recommends pre-employment testing to ensure that employees have the skills necessary to perform the jobs for which they are being hired.

Lindsey, Jonathan A. "Using Negotiation Theory, Conflict Management, and Assertiveness Theory in Performance Evaluation." *Library Administration and Management* 4 (Fall 1990): 195-200. Lindsey provides a useful overview of techniques to use in performance evaluations including negotiation theory, conflict management, and assertiveness theory.

Rubin, Richard. "Evaluation of Reference Personnel" in *Evaluation of Public Services and Public Services Personnel.* Ed. by Bryce Allen, 147-157. Illinois: University of Illinois Urbana-Champaign. 1990. Rubin discusses psychosocial issues related to performance evaluation and describes three evaluation systems that could be used to evaluate reference personnel.

Schwartz, Charles A. "Performance Appraisal: Behavioralism and Its Discontents." *College and Research Libraries* 47 (September 1986): 438-451. Schwartz reviews social science research and theory concerning the effects of behavioralism, minimal model, heurism, and in-house experimentation on performance appraisal. He concludes that libraries must design, test, and implement their own programs of performance appraisal.

Stueart, Robert B., and Barbara B. Moran. "Performance Appraisals" in *Library Management.* 3rd ed. 115-128. Littleton, CO.: Libraries Unlimited, 1987. Stueart and Moran examine the benefits of performance evaluation and indicate how to administer such a program. They discuss awareness of difficulties, methods of performance appraisal, and offer guidelines on conducting a performance appraisal interview.

Williamson, M.G. *Guidelines for Training in Libraries.* Coaching and Counseling Skills, no. 7. London: The Library Association, 1986. Williamson discusses the importance of formal and informal counseling and coaching and outlines the skills needed to successfully conduct these meetings. He includes possible questions to use in a coaching or counseling session.

8 EVALUATION AND REVISION

Chapter Overview

- Reaction Survey
- Testing Performance
- Training Revision
- Developing Trainer's Manual

LOOK FOR —

Things to look for when revising training:
- the successful
- the unsuccessful
- the unnecessary
- the overemphasized
- the omitted

The primary purpose for evaluating training is to determine what needs to be revised in future training programs. If the library or supervisor does not know what sections of the training were unsuccessful, necessary changes will not be made. Conversely, if you do not know what aspects of the training were successful, you may delete or alter them without considering the effects of such an action on the whole training program. When revising training, you need to identify successful, unsuccessful, unnecessary, overemphasized, and omitted tasks. For example, teaching filing rules after the library begins using an online catalog may be irrelevant. Similarly, a library that uses OCLC at the reference desk but does not include training in the use of OCLC may have omitted a very important area of training.

The purpose of evaluating training is to determine whether or not it is effective. You need to know if the paraprofessional is learning what was intended and if the training is being applied on the job. If some aspect of the training program does not work, you need to determine why and revise the training program accordingly. If the training can be demonstrated to be successful—if it clearly makes a difference in the performance of the paraprofessional—then its value becomes self-apparent.

In connection with evaluating the effectiveness of the training program, you need to determine the cost and time of the training program in relation to the end result. If the paraprofessional performs poorly after training, maybe an insufficient amount of time was spent in the training process. The library will ultimately make up for this time in retraining, inefficient service to patrons, or both. The library may decide it cannot afford the amount of time that was spent by the supervisor and trainee; in this case it will need to look for ways to revise the training program to allow more learning to take place on the job rather than in one-on-one sessions between the supervisor and the paraprofessional. You need to consider the cost of supplies as well as staff time used in training the paraprofessional. The library then needs to compare these costs to the value of using paraprofessionals at the reference desk to determine what changes can be made to improve the library's return on its investment.

Evaluation of training also reinforces learning by reviewing what the paraprofessional has been taught. Training evaluation ensures that the paraprofessional thoroughly understands job tasks and the steps involved in them. Areas in which retraining are needed can be identified during training evaluation.

One method of evaluation alone will not accomplish all of these things. Identifying problems and successes in the training program cannot be done solely by testing paraprofessionals or observing their work. The paraprofessional may have learned how to use a source or conduct a reference interview through trial and error or observation rather than as a result of any training that was provided. Because of this, paraprofessionals should not only be asked for their reactions to the training program but should also be tested and observed.

When preparing to evaluate training, you should decide what will be done with the information you receive. This will give the evaluation a focus and increase its usefulness. If problems are identified in the pace of the program, will the program be altered or will the problem be noted but no solution attempted until after the next paraprofessional is trained to see if he or she encounters similar difficulties? Will the information go to the supervisor or to someone higher in the library administration? Will the evaluation be the basis for the decision about whether or not the program should be continued?

This chapter will cover the following aspects of the evaluation and revision of training programs: the reaction survey, performance testing, revision of training, revision of job descriptions, and creation of a trainer's manual.

REACTION SURVEY

TRAINING TIPS

The reaction survey can ask about training

- pace
- content
- organization
- support
- supervisor's assistance

The reaction survey allows the paraprofessional to identify any aspects of the training program with which he or she was uncomfortable, and to point out areas of the program that were particularly helpful. It also emphasizes the importance of the paraprofessional to the training program by involving him or her in the revision process. The reaction survey can ask about pace, content, organization, support, and the supervisor's training abilities. A sample reaction survey is provided in Figure 8-1.

When preparing a reaction survey, you need to consider the best time to administer the survey. Giving the survey immediately after the training allows for an initial response about the pace and organization of the training but is probably too soon to ask paraprofessionals to comment on the content of the training program. For example, paraprofessionals will be able to indicate

Figure 8-1

TRAINING REACTION SURVEY

Your responses to this survey will help the Reference Department to identify strengths and weaknesses in the Reference Assistant Training Program. We would like your reactions to the training you received to help us make improvements in the program. Your answers will be confidential and will not affect your evaluation. Please return your completed evaluation to the Director's Office in the enclosed envelope before December 1.

Rank your response from 1–5 according to the scale for each question, with 1 being most favorable and 5 being least favorable.

1. The amount of material covered was _____   1: too much; 5: too little

2. The amount of time for completing
   the practice questions was _____

3. The handouts were _____   1: helpful; 5: not helpful

4. The practice questions were _____

5. The supervisor/trainer was _____

6. The handouts were _____   1: very easy to understand; 5: very difficult to understand

7. The practice questions were _____

8. The supervisor/trainer was _____

9. The training program is _____   1: too long; 5: too short

10. The supervisor/trainer _____   1: always listens; 5: does not listen

11. The training program is well organized. _____   1: strongly agree; 5: strongly disagree

12. The training was interesting. _____

13. The training helps me do my job. _____

14. The handout/practice questions format was the best way for me to learn about these sources. _____

15. The supervisor/trainer knew subject but could not communicate it. _____

16. When answering reference questions, I feel _____   1: confident; 5: unsure of myself

17. When interpreting catalog records, I feel _____

18. When explaining library policies, I feel _____

19. The supervisor/trainer's instruction in operation of equipment was _____   1: more than adequate; 5: insufficient

20. The supervisor/trainer's instruction in use of reference sources was _____

21. The supervisor/trainer's knowledge of the library was _____

22. The supervisor/trainer's knowledge of the department was _____

23. The supervisor/trainer was _____   1: very approachable; 5: not approachable

Please respond to the following questions. You may use the back of the survey if necessary.

- What changes would you make in the training program? Why?

- What aspects of the training program should not be changed and why?

- What is your overall assessment of the training program?

- What information presented during training have you used on the job?

- What information presented during training has not been used on the job?

- In what areas do you believe you still need training?

if they were overwhelmed by the amount of material presented or if they were confused about the sequence of training. Immediately after training however, paraprofessionals will probably be unable to identify training they needed but did not receive. On the other hand, waiting six months to a year after training is probably too long because paraprofessionals will have forgotten many of the specifics of the training program. They will remember only the best and worst aspects of the training process.

There are several ways around this problem. You can administer two separate surveys, the first about pace and organization, to be given at the end of training, and another about content to be given sometime during the second or third month on the job. Alternatively, you can administer a single survey six to ten weeks after the end of the training program, or administer the same survey twice, once within two to three weeks after training and then again two to three months later.

When developing a survey of paraprofessional reaction to training, there are a number of general guidelines about questionnaire design that should be followed. Questions and directions should be clearly stated and easy to understand. A Likert scale, which allows paraprofessionals to respond in degrees of satisfaction, is preferable to yes-or-no questions. Space for comments should be provided. As much as possible, anonymity should be guaranteed. To encourage their honest response, paraprofessionals should be assured that their responses will not affect their own evaluations. Try to provide quiet, uninterrupted time for the paraprofessional to complete the questionnaire. If only one paraprofessional is trained, the supervisor, or someone higher in the administration, may simply want to meet with the paraprofessional to discuss the training program. A prepared list of questions, similar to those used in a written survey, can be a useful tool for giving the discussion a focus and reminding the interviewer what subjects should be covered.

TESTING PERFORMANCE

While the reaction survey indicates what the paraprofessional thought about the program, it does not identify what the paraprofessional learned. This is done by performance testing. When evaluating training through performance testing, the supervisor must refer to the training objectives. The primary goal of training evaluation at this stage is to determine if the objectives were met. If the objectives were met, then presumably the training worked. If the objectives were met, but the paraprofessional is performing poorly, then the objectives should be re-examined. A training objective for card catalog use in an automated library can lead to poor performance on the part of the paraprofessional, but the paraprofessional might score perfectly on a test of his or her knowledge about card catalog usage. Obviously, the training worked but the objective did not.

The objectives of the training program (discussed in Chapter 2) should provide performance measures that can be used to evaluate training. For example, an objective about familiarity with directories might stipulate that the paraprofessional should identify sources of local addresses within three minutes of the reference interview. If the paraprofessional is unable to do this, you need to find out why. Is the measurement of the objective unrealistic? Is the paraprofessional simply unable to perform as expected? Or can the training be blamed?

The most effective way to measure training effectiveness is through the use of pre- and post-tests. By administering a pretest, the supervisor was able to identify areas in which the paraprofessional needed training. Administering the same test again at the conclusion of the training program will indicate how much the paraprofessional has learned, and can be some guide to the effectiveness of training. (A sample pretest is provided in Chapter 6 within the Subject Catalog Training Module.) While the paraprofessional has been meeting with the supervisor for the training modules, he or she has also been observing at the reference desk and beginning to answer questions and therefore will be learning about sources outside of the training program. The post-test, therefore, should concentrate on the sources covered by the training program. The post-test should accurately reflect the amount of time spent on the topics during training. The post-test also indicates if retraining is needed in any area. A brief example of a post-test is provided in Chapter 4 (see Figure 4-5). The pretest in Chapter 6 could also be used as a post-test.

Before administering the post-test, the supervisor should determine what will be considered an adequate score. Will the training be deemed successful if the paraprofessional merely gets one more right than he or she did on the pre-test? Or, at the other extreme, only when the paraprofessional receives a perfect score on the post-test?

You should not inform the paraprofessionals that they will be evaluated. They might try to "study" for it. You should emphasize that the paraprofessionals are not being tested but rather that the training program is being evaluated. During the evaluation be sure the paraprofessional is given a quiet, uninterrupted atmosphere with plenty of time to complete the work. Encourage him or her to make comments about the training program and suggest revisions that could be made. After administering the post-test, the paraprofessionals should be asked if they believe the evaluation adequately covered the training they received.

The post-test can also be readministered three to twelve months after the conclusion of training to determine if the paraprofessional remembers what he or she was taught and if he or she is using the information on the job. If a significant number of questions in one subject area are answered incorrectly, this may indicate that those sources are rarely used on the job or that the training was ineffective or insufficient. These areas should be discussed with the paraprofessional to determine if the sources are used often enough to warrant inclusion in the training program.

If you have time to observe the paraprofessional at the reference desk, it can be valuable to make notes to yourself about his or her performance as it relates to the training objectives. Is the paraprofessional conducting effective reference interviews? Is the paraprofessional using indexes and tables of contents in reference sources adequately? You might want to make a list of the training objectives or the sources you introduced and note the performance of the paraprofessional with each one. If you have time to do this for several weeks, you may be able to identify areas of training that need to be revised, omitted, or added.

REVISION OF TRAINING

Throughout the evaluation of the training program, the goal has been to determine what changes, if any, are needed. Once activities, personnel, or modules that need to be changed have been identified, you can begin to make changes in preparation for the next paraprofessional. You may decide that your hiring standards should be higher or that fewer responsibilities should be assigned to paraprofessionals.

WHY REVISE?

- new technology
- new sources
- new services
- new service points
- new staff

TURNING THE TABLES

Consider asking another staff member to present a section of training. This will increase the team concept among staff members and provide the paraprofessional with exposure to different perspectives and instructional styles.

Consider asking the paraprofessional to create a training module on a topic of interest to him or her. This will increase his or her familiarity with the topic and the sources.

Changes will be needed in the training program as changes occur in the library. New technology, new sources, new services, new service points, or new staff can lead to alterations in the responsibilities of the paraprofessional. These will have to be reflected in the training program.

Through the reaction survey discussed earlier, paraprofessionals probably suggested ways to improve the training program. Possibly the staff business specialist can provide better training in the use of business sources than the supervisor. Maybe a different form of training is needed. Use of audiovisual materials or a computer assisted instruction program may be more effective in presenting some material. The paraprofessionals may indicate that too much or not enough time was spent on a particular subject, service, or source. You should consider all suggestions and determine what changes need to be made. The suggestions should be carried out, or at least noted so that they can be incorporated in the future.

When revising the training modules, the topics should be examined. Ask yourself if the sources covered are still important, and if the sample questions are still representative of what your patrons ask. Generally the paraprofessional will be able to tell you if one training module seems unnecessary or if some important subject was not covered. A training module detailing how to locate information about Native Americans is probably not needed after local teachers create new lesson plans that eliminate study of this subject. New "pet" questions will arise that may require a training module.

Don't let your training modules become stale or dated. You need to determine if any sources that were included in your handouts are no longer generally used. New sources may be used instead and these should be included. You also need to check the shelves to ensure that the volume is still in the library and that the call number and location are correct on the handouts. The questions and answers should also be verified. New editions may affect the questions and answers.

REVISION OF JOB DESCRIPTION

After the paraprofessional has been on the job for about a year, you can ask the paraprofessional to review his or her job description and comment on whether or not it is accurate. If new responsibilities have been added or others deleted, the job description should be rewritten to reflect these changes. New equipment in the library or the department may affect the responsibilities of the paraprofessional. New service hours or service points may change the job description. The job description should be kept current so that if someone new has to be hired, the library can quickly see exactly what the paraprofessional has been doing.

TRAINER'S MANUAL

Throughout the training, you should keep notes, memos, and articles of importance to the training process. Your overview or outline of the training process should be kept as well. Save copies of all items prepared for use with the paraprofessionals (e.g., training modules, pre- and post-tests, memos, forms, etc.). As the training program progresses, you should make notes to yourself about what to change the next time the training program is used. At the conclusion of the training program and evaluation, you can begin to compile a trainer's manual. This manual can be used to document what the paraprofessional should know, what future paraprofessionals should be taught, and what future supervisors should know and do. In essence, it provides consistency between supervisors.

Your trainer's manual should include the following:

- Copies of the job description of the paraprofessional and supervisor
- Application form
- Form letters sent to applicants
- Form letters or memos sent to paraprofessionals
- Training modules
- Pre- and post-tests
- Evaluation forms, and
- Journal articles of importance
- Any other items developed or used for the training program.

As much narrative as is necessary to explain the use of these items can be included. The trainer's manual will be easiest to use if one item is put on each page, a table of contents and index are included, and a loose-leaf notebook is used to allow insertion or deletion of items.

As with all revision and evaluation, this process is really the first step in starting over. With the information and experience you have gained from training your first paraprofessional or group of paraprofessionals, you are ready to return to Chapter 2 and begin planning again. Each time you train employees the process will be easier because you will have the trainer's manual to guide you, and the training or department manual and training modules available for you and the paraprofessionals to use.

RESOURCES

Birnbrauer, Herman. "Evaluation Techniques that Work." *Training and Development Journal* 41 (July 1987): 52-55. Birnbrauer encourages considering evaluation of training while the training objectives are being written instead of after training is over.

Casteleyn, Mary. "Evaluating Training." In *Handbook of Library Training Practice*, edited by Ray Prytherch, 90-125. Aldershot, Hants, England: Gower, 1986. Casteleyn discusses reasons for conducting, planning, implementing, and analyzing evaluations, as well as who should evaluate. She provides sample training evaluation forms.

Fisher, Harold E., and Ronald Weinberg. "Make Training Accountable: Assess Its Impact." *Personnel Journal* 67 (January 1988): 73-77. Fisher and Weinberg discuss why training should be evaluated and how to develop a valid questionnaire to gather trainee reactions to a training program.

Sullivan, Richard L., and Mary Jo Elenburg. "Performance Testing for Technical Trainers." *Training and Development Journal* 42 (November 1988): 38-40. Sullivan and Elenburg discuss why and how to evaluate technical tasks by performance tests.

CUMULATIVE
BIBLIOGRAPHY

Note: All titles annotated at the ends of each chapter are included in this bibliography, as well as many additional titles of interest.

Aluri, Rao, and Jeffrey W. St. Clair. "Academic Reference Librarians: An Endangered Species?" *The Journal of Academic Librarianship* 4 (May 1978): 82-84.

American Library Association. Office of Intellectual Freedom. *Intellectual Freedom Manual*, 3d ed. Chicago: American Library Association, 1989.

American Library Association. Standards Committee, Reference and Adult Services Division. "A Commitment to Information Services: Developmental Guidelines." *RQ* 18 (Spring 1979): 275-278.

Astbury, Effie C. "Library Technicians and the Reference Service." *Canadian Library Journal* 26 (January-February 1969): 54-57.

Bafundo, Donna R. *In-Service Training Program for Library Paraprofessionals: A Report.* Fairfax, VA: George Mason University, (ERIC ED 207-536) June 1981.

Baker, D. *Guidelines for Training in Libraries.* Vol. 6, *Training Library Assistants.* London: Library Association, 1986.

Benson, Larry D. "Reference Assistant Training: An Integrated Approach." In *Enter, Save, Delete...: Libraries Pioneering Into the Next Century*, edited by Douglas G. Birdsall, 16-43. Emporia, KS: Emporia State University, University Press: 1989.

Berkner, Dimity S. "Library Staff Development Through Performance Appraisal." In *The Management Process: A Selection of Readings for Librarians*, edited by Ruth J. Person, 327-341. Chicago: American Library Association, 1983.

Berwind, Anne May. "Orientation for the Reference Desk." *RSR: Reference Services Review* 19 (1991): 51-54, 70.

Birnbrauer, Herman. "Evaluation Techniques that Work." *Training and Development Journal* 41 (July 1987): 52-55.

Bloom, Stuart P. "Organization of Policy and Procedure Statements." *Journal of Systems Management* 34 (July 1983): 24-27.

Bloom, Stuart P., and Evan L. Dold. "A Guide to Developing a Policies and Procedures Manual." *Management World* 10 (June 1981): 27-31.

Bloomberg, Marty. *Introduction to Public Services for Library Technicians.* 4th ed. Littleton, CO: Libraries Unlimited, 1985.

Boorkman, Jo Anne. "The Policy and Procedure Manual: An Essential Management Resource." *Medical Reference Services Quarterly* 2 (Winter 1983): 41-48.

Bopp, Richard E., and Linda C. Smith, eds. *Reference and Information Services: An Introduction.* Englewood, CO: Libraries Unlimited, 1991.

Brinkerhoff, Robert O. "Making Evaluation More Useful." *Training and Development Journal* 35 (December 1981): 66-70.

Broadwell, Martin M. *The Supervisor and On-The-Job Training.* Reading, MA: Addison-Wesley Publishing Co., Inc., 1986.

Byerly, Greg, Martha Goold, and Ruth Main. "Reference Training Manual." University Libraries, Kent State University, Kent OH, 1980. Photocopy.

Cangemi, Joseph P., and Jeffrey C. Claypool. "Complimentary Interviews: A System for Rewarding Outstanding Employees." *Personnel Journal* 57 (February 1978): 87-90.

Cantor, Jeffrey A. "How to Design, Develop, and Use Performance Tests." *Training and Development Journal* 42 (September 1988): 72-75.

Carver, Deborah A. "Creating Effective Manuals: A Bibliographic Essay." *Library Administration and Management* 4 (Summer 1990): 145-148.

Casteleyn, Mary. *Planning Library Training Programmes*. London: Andre Deutsch, 1981.

————. "Evaluating Training." In *Handbook of Library Training Practice*, edited by Ray Prytherch, 90-125. Aldershot, Hants, England: Gower, 1986.

Chabotar, Kent John. "Designing a Training Evaluation System." *Journal of Library Administration* 1 (Summer 1980): 25-37.

Chandler, Lana J. "Welcoming the New Employee." *Supervision* 47 (October 1985): 14-16, 21.

Chernik, Barbara E. *Introduction to Library Services for Library Technicians*. Littleton, CO: Libraries Unlimited, 1982.

Childress, Schelley H. "Training of Student Assistants in College Libraries: Some Insights and Ideas." *Arkansas Libraries* 44 (March 1987): 25-27.

Christensen, John O., Larry D. Benson, H. Juliene Butler, Blaine H. Hall, and Don H. Howard. "An Evaluation of Reference Desk Service." *College and Research Libraries* 50 (July 1989): 468-483.

Coleman, Kathleen, and Elizabeth Margutti. "Training Nonprofessionals for Reference Service." *RQ* 16 (Spring 1977): 217-219.

Connolly, Susan M. "Integrating Evaluation, Design and Implementation." *Training and Development Journal* 42 (February 1988): 20-23.

Conyers, A. *Guidelines for Training in Libraries*. Vol. 2 *The Evaluation of Staff Training*. 2d ed. London: Library Association, 1986.

Cook, James P. "A Five-Step Program That Keeps Training on Target." *Personnel Journal* 65 (November 1986): 106-114.

Courtois, Martin P., and Lori A. Goetsch. "Use of Nonprofessionals at Reference Desks." *College and Research Libraries* 45 (September 1984): 385-391.

Cowley, John. *Personnel Management in Libraries*. London: Clive Bingley, 1982.

Creth, Sheila D. *Effective On-The-Job Training: Developing Library Human Resources*. Chicago: American Library Association, 1986.

Cubberley, Carol W. "Write Procedures That Work." *Library Journal* 116 (September 15, 1991): 42-45.

Davidson, Jeffrey P. "Starting the New Hire on the Right Foot." *Personnel* 63 (August 1988): 67-71.

Dawkins, Willie Mae, and Jeffrey Jackson. "Enhancing Reference Services: Students as Assistants." *Technicalities* 6 (August 1986): 4-7.

Devine, Judith W. "Considerations in the Management of a Reference Department." In *Reference Services Administration and Management*, edited by Bill Katz and Ruth A. Fraley, 61-70. New York: The Haworth Press, 1982.

Dewey, Barbara I. *Library Jobs: How to Fill Them, How to Find Them*. Phoenix, AZ: Oryx Press, 1987.

Diffie-Couch, Priscilla. "How to Give Feedback." In *Performance Evaluation: A Management Basic for Librarians*, edited by Jonathan A. Lindsey, 37-41. Phoenix: Oryx Press, 1986.

Dixon, Nancy M. "Meet Training's Goals Without Reaction Forms." *Personnel Journal* 66 (August 1987): 108-115.

Driscoll, Alice. "Back to Square One: The Writing of a Reference Policy Statement and Procedures Manual." *The Southeastern Librarian* 31 (Fall 1981): 109-112.

Edmonds, Leslie, and Ellen D. Sutton. "The Reference Interview." In *Reference and Information Services: An Introduction*, edited by Richard E. Bopp and Linda C. Smith, 42-58. Englewood, CO: Libraries Unlimited, 1991.

Eichhorn, Karen. "Portable, Packaged Reference Training." *Public Libraries* 22 (Summer 1983): 76-78.

Emmick, Nancy. "Nonprofessionals on Reference Desks in Academic Libraries." In *Conflicts in Reference Services*, edited by Bill Katz and Ruth A. Fraley, 149-160. New York: The Haworth Press, 1985.

Evans, G. Edward, ed. *Management Techniques for Librarians*, 2d ed. New York: Academic Press, 1983.

————— and Bendict Rugaas. "Another Look at Performance Appraisal in Libraries." In *Performance Evaluation: A Management Basic for Librarians*, edited by Jonathan A. Lindsey, 189-197. Phoenix: Oryx Press, 1986.

Evered, James. "How to Write a Good Job Description." *Supervisory Management* 26 (April 1981): 14-19.

Fisher, Harold E., and Ronald Weinberg. "Make Training Accountable: Assess Its Impact." *Personnel Journal* 67 (January 1988): 73-77.

Flinner, Beatrice E. "A Scenario of the Reference Librarian in a Small University Library." *The Reference Librarian* 19 (1987): 341-358.

Fontaine, France, and Paulette Bernhard for the General Information Programme and UNISIST. *Guidelines for Writing Learning Objectives in Librarianship, Information Science and Archives Administration.* Paris: UNESCO, 1988.

Freides, Thelma. "Current Trends in Academic Libraries." *Library Trends* 31 (Winter 1983): 457-474.

Fulton, Tara Lynn. "Reference Librarianship: Sharing Our Knowledge With Technical Service Colleagues." *RQ* 27 (Winter 1987): 210-219.

Futas, Elizabeth. *The Library Forms Illustrated Handbook.* New York: Neal-Schuman, 1984.

Gates, Jean Key. *Guide to the Use of Libraries and Information Sources.* 6th ed. New York: McGraw-Hill, 1989.

Gibbs, Sally. "Staff Appraisal." In *Handbook of Library Training Practice*, edited by Ray Prytherch, 61-81. Aldershot, Hants, England: Gower, 1986.

Glogoff, Stuart, and James P. Flynn. "Developing a Systematic In-House Training Program for Integrated Library Systems." *College and Research Libraries* 48 (November 1987): 528-536.

Glover, Peggy. "Updating a Reference Services Policy Statement." In *Reference Services Administration and Management*, edited by Bill Katz and Ruth A. Fraley, 51-54. New York: Haworth Press, 1982.

Golden, Fay Ann. "The Ethics of Reference Service for the Public Librarian." *The Reference Librarian* 30 (1990): 157-166.

Goldfarb, Stephen M. "Writing Policies and Procedures Manuals." *Journal of Systems Management* 32 (April 1981): 10-12.

Gothberg, Helen M. "Managing Difficult People: Patrons (and Others)." *The Reference Librarian* 19 (1987): 269-283.

Goulding, Mary. "Real Librarians Don't Play 'Jeopardy'." *Illinois Libraries* 73 (February 1991): 140-146.

Grant, Philip C. "What Use is a Job Description?" *Personnel Journal* 67 (February 1988): 45-53.

Graves, J. Peter. "Let's Put Appraisal Back in Performance Appraisal: Part I." In *Performance Evaluation: A Management Basic for Librarians*, edited by Jonathan A. Lindsey, 131-140. Phoenix: Oryx Press, 1986.

————. "Let's Put Appraisal Back in Performance Appraisal: Part II." In *Performance Evaluation: A Management Basic for Librarians*, edited by Jonathan A. Lindsey, 141-149. Phoenix: Oryx Press, 1986.

"Guidelines for Medical, Legal and Business Responses at General Reference Desks." *RQ* 31 (Summer 1992): 554-555.

Guy, Jeniece. *Writing Library Job Descriptions*. Chicago: American Library Association, Office for Library Personnel Resources, 1985. T.I.P. Kit #7.

Halatin, T.J. "Evaluating the Superior Employee." In *Performance Evaluation: A Management Basic for Librarians*, edited by Jonathan A. Lindsey, 109-112. Phoenix: Oryx Press, 1986.

Hauer, Mary G., et al. *Books, Libraries, and Research*. 3d ed. Dubuque, IA: Kendall-Hunt, 1990.

Haynes, Marion E. "Developing an Appraisal Program, Part I." *Personnel Journal* 57 (January 1978): 14-19.

———. "Developing an Appraisal Program, Part II." *Personnel Journal* 57 (February 1978), 66-7, 104, 107.

Hendley, Margaret. "Staff Training in an Automated Environment." *Canadian Library Journal* 46 (April 1989): 101-103.

Hilton, Robert C. "Performance Evaluation of Library Personnel." *Special Libraries* 6 (November 1978): 429-434.

Hoffman, Frank W. "Procedure Manuals in Librarianship." In *Encyclopedia of Library and Information Science*, edited by Allen Kent, 339-348. Volume 38. Suppl. 3. New York: Marcel Dekker, 1985.

InfoTrac: General Periodicals Index. Foster City, CA: Information Access Company, 1993.

Isenstein, Laura J. "Get Your Reference Staff on the STAR Track." *Library Journal* 117 (April 15, 1992): 34-37.

———. "On the Road to STARdom." *Illinois Libraries* 73 (February 1991): 146-151.

Jennerich, Elaine Zaremba, and Edward J. Jennerich. *The Reference Interview as a Creative Art*. Littleton, CO: Libraries Unlimited, Inc., 1987.

Jones, Dorothy E. "I'd Like You to Meet Our New Librarian: The Initiation and Integration of the Newly Appointed Librarian." *The Journal of Academic Librarianship* 14 (September 1988): 221-224.

Jones, Noragh, and Peter Jordan. *Staff Management in Library and Information Work.* 2d ed. Hants, England: Gower, 1987.

Jordan, Peter. "Training in Handling Users." In *Handbook of Library Training Practice*, edited by Ray Prytherch, 167-190. Aldershot, Hants, England: Gower, 1986.

Kathman, Michael D., and Jane M. Kathman. "Integrating Student Employees into the Management Structure of Academic Libraries." *Catholic Library World* 56 (March 1985): 328-331.

Katz, William A. *Introduction to Reference Work.* Vol 2. *Reference Service and Reference Processes.* 4th ed. New York: McGraw Hill, 1983.

Kikoski, John F., and Joseph A. Litterer. "Effective Communication in the Performance Appraisal Interview." In *Performance Evaluation: A Management Basic for Librarians*, edited by Jonathan A. Lindsey, 23-36. Phoenix: Oryx Press, 1986.

Knight, Aldis M. "How To Establish Standards and Expectations." Supervisory Skills Series, Career Development/Personnel Services, Purdue University, West Lafayette, IN, March 21, 1989. Handout.

Komras, Henrietta. "Evaluating Your Training Programs." *Training and Development Journal* 39 (September 1985): 87-88.

Lindsey, Jonathan A. "The Human Dimension in Performance Appraisal." In *Performance Evaluation: A Management Basic for Librarians*, edited by Jonathan A. Lindsey, 3-8. Phoenix: Oryx Press, 1986.

Lindsey, Jonathan A. "Using Negotiation Theory, Conflict Management, and Assertiveness Theory in Performance Evaluation." *Library Administration and Management* 4 (Fall 1990): 195-200.

Loraine, Kaye. "Taking the Pain Out of Orientation." *Supervision* 50 (May 1988): 3-5.

Luccock, Graham. "Induction Training." In *Handbook of Library Training Practice*, edited by Ray Prytherch, 3-36. Aldershot, Hants, England: Gower, 1986.

McCarthy, Constance. "Paraprofessionals, Student Assistants, and the Reference Clan: An Application of Contemporary Management Theory," in *Academic Libraries: Myths and Realities: Proceedings of the Third National Conference of the Association of College and Research Libraries.* edited by Suzanne C. Dodson and Gary L. Menges, 382-386. Chicago: Association of College and Research Libraries, 1984.

McMurry, Nan. "From Library Student to Library Professional: Smoothing the Transition for the New Librarian." *North Carolina Libraries* 49 (Winter 1988): 209-213.

Mager, Robert. *Preparing Instructional Objectives*. 2d ed. Belmont, CA: Pitman Learning, 1975.

Matthis, Leslie H. "Writing Your First Procedure—How to Go About It." *Journal of Systems Management* 38 (November 1987): 25-29.

Miller, Mary Jane. "Constructing Job Descriptions for Library Support Staff Positions: a Modular Approach." In *Managing the Electronic Library*, edited by Michael Koenig, 32-45. New York: Special Libraries Association, 1983.

Minney, Marilyn, and Pamela Bradigan. "Training and Orientation of a Newly Hired Reference Librarian." Ohio Library Association, Columbus, October 1988. Handout.

Montag, John. "Choosing How to Staff the Reference Desk." In *Personnel Issues in Reference Services*, edited by Bill Katz and Ruth A. Fraley, 31-37. New York: The Haworth Press, 1986.

Mosby, Anne Page, and Glenda Hughes. "Continuing Education for Librarians—Training for Online Searching." *The Reference Librarian* 30 (1990): 105-118.

Moss, Karen M. "The Reference Communication Process." *Law Library Journal* 72 (Winter 1979): 48-52.

Mugnier, Charlotte. *The Paraprofessional and the Professional Job Structure*. Chicago: American Library Association, 1980.

Murfin, Marjorie E., and Charles A. Bunge. "Paraprofessionals at the Reference Desk." *The Journal of Academic Librarianship* 14 (March 1988): 10-14.

Murfin, Marjorie. "Trends in Use of Support Staff and Students at the Reference Desk in Academic Libraries." *Library Personnel News* 2 (Winter 1988): 10-12.

Neville, Sandra H. "Day to Day Management of Reference Service." In *Reference Services Administration and Management*, edited by Bill Katz and Ruth A. Fraley, 15-27. New York: The Haworth Press, 1982.

Newstrom, John W. *Games Trainers Play*. New York: McGraw-Hill, 1980.

———. *More Games Trainers Play*. New York: McGraw-Hill, 1983.

Nichols, Margaret Irby. "The Reference Services Policy Manual." *Texas Library Journal* 63 (Spring 1987): 30-32.

Nolan, Christopher W. "Closing the Reference Interview: Implications for Policy and Practice." *RQ* 31 (Summer 1992): 513-523.

"Off to a Good Start: A Checklist for the Training of the New Librarian." *Ohio Libraries* 3 (January/February 1990): 6-7.

Ohles, Judith K. *Training Coordinator's Manual: A Handbook for Training Preprofessionals at a Reference Desk*. Kent, OH: Kent State University, (ERIC ED 301-221) 1988.

Performance Appraisal. Washington, D.C.: Association of Research Libraries. Systems and Procedures Exchange Center, 1979.

Preece, Barbara G., and Betty J. Glass. "The Online Catalog and Staff Training." *Library Software Review* 10 (March/April 1991): 100-104.

Reference Policies and Procedures Manual. Fairfax, VA: George Mason University, 1980. ERIC ED 185-975

Ricks, Thomas, et al. "Finding the Real Information Need: An Evaluation of Reference Negotiation Skills." *Public Libraries* 30 (May/June 1991): 159-164.

Rider, Lillian M. *Training Program for Reference Desk Staff*. 2d ed. Montreal, Canada: Montreal Reference Department, McLennon Library, McGill University, 1979. ERIC ED 175-486.

Rolstad, Gary O. "Training Adult Services Librarians." *RQ* 27 (Summer 1988): 474-477.

Roman, Susan. "The Performance Appraisal: A Positive Process." *Illinois Libraries* 64 (December 1982): 1175-1177.

Rooks, Dana C. *Motivating Today's Library Staff*. Phoenix, AZ: Oryx Press, 1988.

Ross, Catherine Sheldrick, and Patricia Dewdney. *Communicating Professionally*. New York: Neal-Schuman Publishers. 1989.

Rubin, Richard. "Evaluation of Reference Personnel." In *Evaluation of Public Services and Public Services Personnel*, edited by Bryce Allen, 147-157. Illinois: University of Illinois Urbana-Champaign, 1990.

———. *Human Resource Management in Libraries*. New York: Neal-Schuman Publishers, 1991.

Ryan, Kathleen, and Peggy Royster. "The Procedure Manual." In *The How-To-Do-It Manual for Small Libraries*, edited by Bill Katz, 132-140. New York: Neal-Schuman, 1988.

St. Clair, Jeffrey W., and Rao Aluri. "Staffing the Reference Desk: Professionals or Nonprofessionals?" *The Journal of Academic Librarianship* 3 (July 1977): 149-153.

Schippleck, Suzanne. *Library Reference Service.* Inglewood, CA: Inglewood Public Library, 1976.

Schlessinger, Bernard S., and June H. Schlessinger. "The Ten Commandments for Performance Appraisal Interviews." In *Performance Evaluation: A Management Basic for Librarians,* edited by Jonathan A. Lindsey, 9-13. Phoenix: Oryx Press, 1986.

Schwartz, Charles A. "Performance Appraisal: Behavioralism and Its Discontents." *College and Research Libraries* 47 (September 1986): 438-451.

Schwartz, Diane G., and Dottie Eakin. "Reference Service Standards, Performance Criteria, and Evaluation." *The Journal of Academic Librarianship* 12 (March 1986): 4-8.

Slavens, Thomas P. *Informational Interviews and Questions.* Metuchen, NJ: The Scarecrow Press, Inc. 1978.

Smith, Ronald E. "Employee Orientation: 10 Steps to Success." *Personnel Journal* 63 (December 1984): 46-48.

Stabler, Karen. "Introductory Training of Academic Reference Librarians: A Survey." *RQ* 26 (Spring 1987): 363-369.

Stanley, Suzanne. "Information Sources." In *Handbook of Library Training Practice,* edited by Ray Prytherch, 207-277. Aldershot, Hants, England: Gower, 1986.

Strubbe, Lisa Aren, and Diane G. Schwartz. "A Two-Year MLS Internship Program." *College and Research Libraries News* 49 (September 1988): 504-508.

Stueart, Robert B., and Barbara B. Moran. *Library Management.* 3d ed. Littleton, CO: Libraries Unlimited, 1987.

Sullivan, Richard L., and Mary Jo Elenburg. "Performance Testing for Technical Trainers." *Training and Development Journal* 42 (November 1988): 38-40.

Taylor, Margaret T., and Ronald R. Powell. *Basic Reference Sources: A Self-Study Manual.* 4th ed. Metuchen, NJ: The Scarecrow Press, 1990.

Tracey, William R. *Designing Training and Development Systems.* New York: AMACOM, 1984.

Travers, Alfred W. *Supervision: Techniques and New Dimensions.* Englewood Cliffs, NJ: 1988.

Wade, Gordon S. "Managing Reference Services in the Smaller Public Library." In *Reference Services Administration and Management,* edited by Bill Katz and Ruth A. Fraley, 107-112. New York: The Haworth Press, 1982.

Wagel, William H. "Making New Hires Part of the Company." *Personnel* 63 (May 1986): 4-6.

Williamson, M.G. *Guidelines for Training in Libraries.* Vol. 7 *Coaching and Counseling Skills.* London: The Library Association, 1986.

Woodard, Beth S. "The Effectiveness of an Information Desk Staffed by Graduate Students and Nonprofessionals." *College and Research Libraries* 50 (July 1989): 455-467.

———. "Training, Development, and Continuing Education for the Reference Staff." In *Reference and Information Services: An Introduction,* edited by Richard E. Bopp and Linda C. Smith, 151-170. Englewood, CO: Libraries Unlimited, 1991.

Woodard, Beth S., and Sharon J. Van Der Laan. "Training Preprofessionals for Reference Service." In *Reference Services Today: From Interview to Burnout,* edited by Bill Katz and Ruth A. Fraley, 233-254. New York: The Haworth Press, 1986.

Yates, Rochelle. *A Librarian's Guide to Telephone Reference Service.* Hamden, CT: Library Professional Publications, 1986.

INDEX

Julie Ann McDaniel is the Public Services Librarian at Ohio Wesleyan University in Delaware, Ohio.

Judith K. Ohles is Director of the Kent State University Library at Stark Campus in Canton, Ohio.

Book design: Gloria Brown
Cover design: Gregory Apicella
Typography: Benchmark Productions, Inc.